HERE AND THERE

Tom Symalla

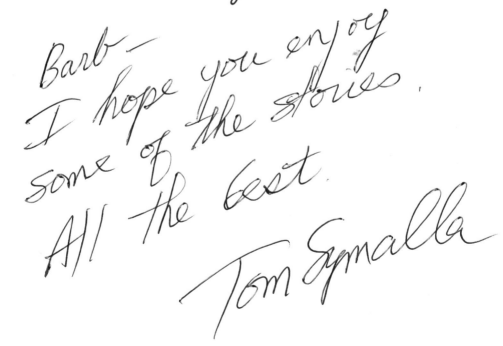

Barb —
I hope you enjoy
some of the stories.
All the best.
Tom Symalla

Copyright © 2009 by Tom M. Symalla.

All rights reserved. No part of this book may be reproduced in any means, mechanical or electronic, except for brief passages to be used in critical reviews.

Please note that this book is a work of fiction. Names, characters, places, and events are either the product of the author's imagination, or, if real, are used fictitiously. Any actual resemblance to actual persons, places, or names may be completely coincidental.

ISBN #1441466363

For my family.

Acknowledgments

As someone who reads a lot of books, I've noted that real authors can dedicate books to just one person and be done with it. To me, this means that they've either written a book before or they plan to write another.

When I was a kid growing up in Cold Spring, Minnesota, Vikings coach Bud Grant would prohibit his football players from the touchdown celebrations that have become so commonplace in the NFL. Grant would tell his players to act like they'd been there before. No need to celebrate if you had expected to get to the end zone. No need to celebrate if you expected to get there again. It was a simple rule that made a lot of sense. Act like you've been there before.

Well, because I haven't written a book before and because it took me over 30 years to write this one, I figure I better get in all of my acknowledgments now. Please pardon the longevity.

To Mary Riebe, Karlyn Elgin, Mary Jo Fibuch, and Dee Dee Ward, friends and co-workers when I was fresh out of college many, many years ago. Back then, I talked way too often about my dream of someday writing a book. It would have been easy for any of you to douse my aspirations, especially since I spent more time talking about writing a book than I spent writing it. To all of you: Even though the years have passed, you should know that your faith in me was never forgotten. Although we haven't all kept in touch, I know you're out there somewhere and I hope all is well.

To the Reverend James Whalen, a journalism professor at the College of St. Thomas. To Catherine Lupori, a creative writing professor at the College of St. Catherine. To Florence Meyer, an English teacher at Rocori High School. You were all teachers who encouraged me to believe in myself. You were all teachers who made a difference.

To my friend and business associate Denise Chambers. Throughout the many years we've worked together, you've been subjected to many of the stories which appear in this book. You've been a captive audience of sorts, maybe because I sign your paycheck. I'm sure you've heard some of these stories so many times that you could probably tell them better than I can. Thanks for always listening.

And to friend and former business associate Kelly Boone: Although you weren't forced to listen to many of the same stories, you often had to listen to me talk about my hope to someday finish my book. You were always supportive; I appreciated the kindness and the optimism.

And to my grandfathers, Grandpa Symalla and Grandpa Witschen: Most kids are lucky to have one grandfather to admire. I had two. Some of my fondest childhood memories are of my grandpa and namesake Tom Symalla and the stories he told to an eager collection of grandchildren around his kitchen table. As he stoked and toked a pipe full of Prince Albert tobacco or as he downed his daily jigger of Christian Brothers brandy, Grandpa Symalla regaled and entertained us with a repertoire of tales. When he couldn't think of a word, he'd replace it with "whatyacallit" or "thingamajig". We almost always knew what he meant. When we didn't, Grandma would interpret. Grandpa Symalla taught me the value of a good story. The stories he told and the way he told them made a lasting impression on me. I've forgotten some of the stories, but I've not forgotten how entertaining they were.

And to my other grandfather, Vincent Witschen. He was a different kind of hero. I didn't get to see him as much as my other grandpa, because he lived further away, And I didn't realize that he was the special person he was until after he died. A surviving member of "The Lost Battalion" in World War I, Grandpa Witschen was one of 800 soldiers trapped behind enemy lines and under siege by German troops in France's Argonne Forest. Without food, water, ammunition, or medical supplies, only 200 U.S. soldiers survived this suicidal mission. Grandpa Witschen never let his war experiences affect his faith, his hope, or his charity. He had a heart of gold. He would be happy to know that his love for baseball lives on in many of his daughters and some of his grandchildren. The love of baseball. We will always have that in common.

And finally, to my family: My Mom. My Dad. My sister Barb. My sister Joan. Although some of the stories in this book will indicate that I'm a bit too willing to air the family's dirty laundry, you should know that my intentions are good and I hope some of the stories will bring back memories of the happy household we shared. We've all remained close friends as time has passed and that means a lot to me. I love you all.

Before we get started

As you read this book, you should know that I've taken some liberties with some of the characters and some of the events. I've changed some names to protect the innocent. I've changed other names to protect the guilty. Some names have remained the same, either because there was no imminent threat of a lawsuit or because I thought a friend or family member might get a kick out of having his or her name mentioned in a book that might sell 75 copies.

Although my intentions were good in recalling stories from my childhood through adulthood, I'm finding that my memory isn't what it used to be and I can now barely remember my way to the bathroom in the morning.

So, as the legal beagles would say, any resemblances to actual persons or places described herein may be purely coincidental.

Throughout the years, when I've told friends or family of my interest in writing a book, many of them have asked, "Why?" Unfortunately, some of you may be asking the same question after you've read this book. For those of you who feel this way after finishing or trying to finish my book, I offer the following reminder: "All Sales Are Final!" Or, in other words, "I Got Your Money, Sucka!"

Finally, on a more serious note, as you read this book, you should know that I'll consider it a success if you are entertained or impacted by any of the stories. In this day and age when dysfunctional lives or stories are considered fodder for good books, I'm happy to say that I can't offer that. I realize that this may not make me a candidate to write a book, or worse, for anyone to read it. But that's neither here nor there. Enjoy!

Contents

Hide the Popsicles

The events of a summer's night left me questioning my manhood.

It had been a long week and I was happy to be home alone. Before reacquainting myself with my recliner, I changed into a pair of sweatpants, grabbed a beer, and the remote control. Turning on the television, I was ready for a night of mindless drivel.

After a round of channel-surfing, I settled upon NBC's "Providence", probably the first indication that I should have been questioning my manhood. The veterinarian on the show was treating an old dog with a gas problem, and that was mindless enough for me.

Then it happened. In my own home, I was forced to confront one of the fears and phobias that had haunted me since childhood. When the intruder appeared out of nowhere, I realized I wasn't alone in my living room. Flying around my house, unlike the previous year's intruder, it was silent. Immediately, I knew what it was.

Just the year before, as I'd entered my home in a semi-comatose I'm-glad-this-day-is-done state of mind, I'd surprised a wayward swallow that had entered through my chimney. The screeching bird was terrified and it quickly proceeded to shit on most of my valued belongings: my Roger Staubach autographed football, my Nolan Ryan autographed baseball, my Santana Abraxas album cover, my Octoberfest beer stein, and a navy pinstripe suit coat that I hoped would someday fit again.

Within minutes of my appearance, the scared bird had left his own autograph on many of my belongings. I never knew a small animal could have so much shit. By the time I'd eventually scared him shitless, I finally figured out that I could enable his exodus by opening the patio door. I did and he was quickly gone.

This year's intruder was a lot more quiet. When it didn't squawk, chirp, or screech, my deepest fears were realized. There was a bat loose in the house. As a kid, I'd been terrified of bats. When I spilled the beer I'd just opened in my lap, I realized I was still terrified of bats.

In a knee-jerk reaction, I bolted into the bathroom and locked the door. (Yeah, as if a bat was going to be able to open the door.) I hadn't personally encountered a bat before, but I had memories of my mom going ballistic when she discovered a bat thrashing about in a wastebasket in our house when I was a young boy.

As my mom yelled and screamed, she designated my dad to get rid of the brown furry creature. As man of the house, this came with the territory for my dad. I was glad I was just a kid and I wasn't sure I ever wanted those responsibilities. My dad calmly covered the wastebasket with a deskpad and then deposited the bat in our backyard.

Now, trapped by fear in my own bathroom, my mind was racing. Everything I knew about bats was going through my head: "Blind as a bat", bats will fly into your hair (no worries there), bats carry rabies, a guy in St. Cloud had recently been bitten by a bat as he slept and the guy had to get rabies shots.

On a lighter note, I wondered if it was an Ecuadorian Sac-Winged Bat, a Rare Florida Mastiff Bat, or a Honduran Fruit-Eating Bat. If it was a fruit-eating bat, I wondered if it would go after the grape popsicles I had hoped to have for dinner that night as part of my latest nutrition kick to achieve the five recommended daily servings of fruits and vegetables.

As I tried to muster the courage to reclaim my territory, I wondered what had ever happened to the Tom who had caught and played with snakes as a kid. I was a shadow of my former self, and speaking of shadows, I was apparently afraid of my own.

My choice of weapons in the bathroom was limited. I opted for a large bath towel and doused it with water. I also decided to go straight from the bathroom to the hall closet to arm myself with a broom. I wasn't sure if I remembered what a broom looked like, because I never used it to clean, but I identified it immediately.

Broom in one hand and wet towel in the other, I entered the living room as a warrior, albeit a timid one. My guest again stirred. He may have been taunting me as he flew around the room and I continually missed him with the towel and the broom. Finally, he got tired of flying and landed on the carpet behind the TV.

Immediately, I laid the heavy wet towel on him, eliciting a series of squeaks and hisses…from me, not the bat.

I had to decide what to do with the bat. My first thought was to try to kill it by stepping on the towel or by jabbing the towel with the broom handle.

But then I realized that I didn't have it in me to kill the thing. As much as I was terrified of bats, I couldn't bring myself to kill the tiny creature. I flashed back to fourth grade science when Miss Sorensten had taught us that bats are our friends. They could eat as many as 1000 to 2000 mosquitoes an hour...and they wouldn't fly into your hair.

I imagined how frightened this little mammal must be, trapped under a towel by a mammoth creature who had been watching a TV show about a dog with gas.

I grabbed an empty water pitcher and a magazine and slow-ly lifted the towel. Carefully, I got the bewildered bat to crawl into the pitcher. Covered with the magazine, I walked the pitcher to my patio, where I released my visitor. He crawled, then flew away.

As I watched him fly into the night, I knew I'd think of him next time I was bitten by a mosquito...and I'd wonder why he wasn't doing his job. I was embarrassed at how scared I'd been; I realized I'd never be afraid of bats again. Maybe the best way to overcome my fear was to be confronted with it.

Lessons Learned Well,
Dr. Spock or Not

A friend of mine recently told a story. He and his wife invited a couple they'd become newly acquainted with into their home for a Saturday night dinner. For my friend Tim and his wife Julie, this dinner was their first social outing with the couple they'd met through their son Brandon's kindergarten class. Brandon had become quick friends with the other couple's son and the sets of parents also became hi-how-are-you familiar.

As long as the boys were going to be friends, Tim and Julie thought they'd expand their circle of friends. After all, the other couple seemed nice enough and a mutual friendship offered the chance to compare notes about kindergarten and other things of common interest.

Just before Tim and Julie's guests arrived for dinner, Brandon had wandered to a neighbor's house without telling his folks. Young Brandon had been told umpteen times that he wasn't to leave home unless he had received permission from Tim or Julie. When Tim and Julie had scoured the neighborhood in search of their missing young son, they found him where they usually found him, at his friend Nick's house.

After they had all returned home, Tim administered a mild spanking to young Brandon and then sent him to his room.

Neither Tim nor Julie were gung-ho about spankings, but it appeared to be one of the few ways to get through to their five-year-old son.

When Tim and Julie's dinner guests had inquired about Brandon's whereabouts, Tim was quick to relate the entire story to them as the two couples had pre-dinner drinks and conversation. When Tim got to the spanking part of the story, he could immediately sense that the tone of the evening had changed. The other couple was aghast and appalled that Tim had spanked his kid. They would never hit their child, they said. It just wasn't good parenting.

Tim politely tried to explain that he hadn't beaten his son. Tim's father had spanked him and Tim had turned out OK, he jokingly pointed out to the other couple. Sometimes it seemed like spankings were the only way to get Brandon's attention.

To make a long story short, Tim's story of spanking Brandon quickly escalated into a full-blown philosophical discussion on parenting, despite Tim's attempt to steer the conversation in a different direction. The conversation eventually became heated and the other couple decided they did not want to share dinner with Tim and Julie. As Tim described it, there were plenty of pot roast and potatoes left over from a meal that was never served. Neither Tim nor Julie was hungry after the abrupt departure of their dinner guests.

Although Dr. Benjamin Spock's bible on parenting was available when I was a kid, my parents opted to trust their instincts instead. It was something that had worked for their parents and for their parents' parents. They would do what they thought would work best.

As a kid, at least until I was 10 or 11, Trouble was my middle name. Oh, I wasn't a bad kid, but I liked to test the limits of my parents' patience. In response, my parents sometimes chose to use dramatic measures to curb my wayward behavior. I'll be the first to admit that verbal reprimands or simple scolding often went in one ear and out the other.

When I came home from grade school with my first swear words, I was politely reminded that those words were not spoken in our house, unless my dad was trying to assemble our Christmas presents.

I didn't heed my mom's warnings. I continued to use bad language in front of my younger sisters and I became quite proficient at it.

My mom tried lectures, go-to-your-room punishments, and groundings, but I continued to spew obscenities throughout the household. I fancied myself a wordsmith, I had learned some new words, and I was bound and determined that anyone within earshot would hear my new cuss words.

Mom got tired of my act. When she had finally had enough, she ushered me by my collar into the family bathroom, where she intended to end this habit once and for all. Grabbing the bar of Ivory soap from the soap dish, she announced her plans to wash my filthy mouth with soap. My younger sisters formed an eager audience in the hallway.

These were days before they had the good-tasting soaps like Irish Spring, Coast, and Zest.

As Mom tried again and again to force the bar of Ivory soap into the mouth that swore, I promised again and again to clean up my language. As my mom persisted, I finally put an end to the charade by biting a chunk out of the bar of soap.

"There. Does that make you happy?", I glared at my mom.

"Well, now you've ruined a good bar of soap. I just wanted you to get a taste of it. You're not supposed to chew the soap. You could get sick from doing that. Thomas Michael, what's wrong with you?"

"Well, how am I supposed to taste the soap if I don't chew it?"

"Enough of that, young man. Don't raise your voice to me. Are you going to stop swearing now? We will not tolerate that language in this household. Do you understand?"

"I suppose."

I'll admit that the Ivory soap didn't taste very good, but it wasn't any worse than the beets and rutabaga I was sometimes forced to eat.

The bottom line: I stopped swearing, at least until I got to college, and I've never sworn much since. In remembrance of my days as a kid, however, I still enjoy a small jigger of liquid soap before I go to bed every night. Seems I've acquired a taste for the stuff. It helps me sleep better, I blow bubbles when I snore, and when I wake up in the morning, my breath is zestful-ly clean.

Much to his dismay, my dad also played an active role in my childhood discipline.

When I was eight years old, baseball was more important than life itself. When I wasn't playing baseball a couple of times a day, I was watching Twins games on the television or listening to them on the radio. For the late-night Twins games against the Los Angeles Angels, I'd sneak my small transistor radio under my bed covers and listen pitch-by-pitch.

My mom had told me not to listen to the entire game, but she knew better.

"I wonder who won the Twins game last night?", she'd ask over breakfast.

"I'm not sure, but I dreamt that the Twins won 4-3", I'd answer excitedly. "Killebrew hit a homerun in the eighth. And Allison hit a run-scoring double. Pascual went the distance, complete game."

"Isn't it funny how your dreams seem to match what actually happened in the game. I just heard the recap on WCCO and the game appears to be identical to your dream. That's remarkable. Are you sure you don't have some kind of gift?", Mom asked with a knowing smile. "I thought I told you not to listen to the entire game. You need your sleep, young man."

When I wasn't playing baseball and when the Twins weren't playing, I'd bike up to the Cold Spring Municipal Ballpark, where I'd watch the Cold Spring Springers town ball team take on teams from the neighboring towns, sometimes even from other parts of the state.

Baseball in my blood, baseball on the brain, I also collected and traded Topps baseball cards.

Rieland's Rexall Drug Store was one of the few places in Cold Spring that sold baseball cards, which came five cards and a stick of bubblegum to a pack. Rieland's Rexall was about a block from St. Boniface School and I passed the store every day on my walk home.

The baseball cards were displayed near the entrance of the drug store on the candy rack. Whenever I had a nickel, I'd buy a pack of cards. Whenever I didn't have a nickel, I'd wait until Mr. Rieland was busy filling a prescription and then I'd stick a couple packs in my pocket. Growing up as a Catholic, I knew this was considered a venial sin and the punishment prescribed during Confession was usually 10 Hail Mary's and an Our Father. This was the going rate from Father Elmer and it was well worth the chance for a Tony Oliva rookie card.

I found out quickly that if I ganged my sins, the penance would almost always be the same. Apparently, there wasn't much of a penalty for multiple sins, as long as they were venial.

"Bless me, Father, for I have sinned. It's been three weeks since my last confession. These are my sins: I fought with my sisters eight times, maybe nine. I disobeyed my parents five times that I can remember. I lied maybe four or five times. I wished my parents would put me up for adoption once, but then I changed my mind when they promised to take me to a Twins-Yankees game, so I don't know if that counts as a sin. And I also stole some baseball cards from the drug store. Your leniency in administering my penance will be deeply appreciated."

After Father Elmer had lectured me about my transgressions, he assigned a penance of 10 Hail Mary's and an Our Father and encouraged me to "go in peace to love and serve the Lord".

Well, my five-finger discounts at Rieland's Rexall went on until I'd assembled one of the largest baseball card collections in Cold Spring. I had Keds shoeboxes full of cards and I'd log these player-by-player and team-by-team on index cards which I paid for with my allowance. Billy Kaufman and Tom Wirtzfeld and I would get together sometimes to flaunt our collections and trade cards. They'd obtained their cards legally.

When Mr. Rieland called my dad and told him that I'd been lifting baseball cards from his store for quite some time, my dad was livid. Dad was a route salesman and sold boxes of Brach's candies to Mr. Rieland. Embarrassed to learn that his young son was jeopardizing his business relationship with Mr. Rieland and disappointed to find out that his son was a budding criminal, Dad drove me immediately to Mr. Rieland's drug store.

On a Saturday morning, Dad excused our way to the front of the line past a half-dozen curious customers who were awaiting their turn at the counter. The customers were initially irritated that we'd broken in line, but they became tolerant when they realized they were in for some unexpected entertainment.

My dad stood behind me as I apologized to Mr. Rieland, who seemed like a nice man and didn't deserve to be the victim of my thievery. He worked hard for his money, my dad said, and I had no right to steal from him.

As I talked, I looked at the floor, hoping to find a hole to crawl into, but Dad reminded me to be a man and look at Mr. Rieland when I talked. I told Mr. Rieland that I was sorry for stealing from him, I told him I hoped that he would continue to buy candies from my dad who had nothing to do with my stealing, and I told Mr. Rieland that I hoped he wouldn't call Mr. Cheeley, the town sheriff.

When I had finished apologizing, Mr. Rieland asked me how many cards I'd stolen.

"I'm not sure, sir", I answered, "but I suppose it's two or three thousand."

Even Mr. Rieland was surprised. "That's an awful lot of cards, young man."

"Yes, sir. I suppose it is", I admitted. I didn't have the courage to look back at the captivated customers who were in line behind me, but I was sure that I'd never be able to walk the streets of Cold Spring again without someone pointing and saying, "There goes that Symalla boy."

Mr. Rieland did some calculating with his pad and pencil. My dad had already pulled out his wallet with the idea he would pay Mr. Rieland immediately for my improprieties and then when we got home, he would take it out of my hide and my allowance.

"That could be up to $30 worth of cards, young man", Mr. Rieland looked at me sternly from behind the counter at the same time my dad quietly tucked his wallet back into his pants, probably realizing that he didn't have that much money in his wallet.

Dad assured Mr. Rieland that I would go to the First National Bank first thing Monday morning to withdraw money from my savings account. I would pay Mr. Rieland the money I owed him and I would never steal from him again. "Isn't that right, son?"

"Yes, sir. I'm sorry, Mr. Rieland. I promise I won't steal from you again."

Bottom line: It was a lesson I'll never forget. I don't think I ever stole anything again, at least not until college when alcohol and I got involved in the heist of imprinted barware from a Wisconsin drinking establishment. I don't know how Dr. Spock would have handled the matter of the stolen baseball cards, but I doubt he could have handled it better than my father.

What Do You Think I Am?
A Moron?

It seemed like forever, but the 3 o'clock bell finally signaled the end of the school day.

My algebra book closed concurrently as Mr. Kearin barked out a reminder about that night's homework assignment.

"I'll pick you up in about 15 minutes", I informed Hans as we bolted out of the classroom. "I just gotta change my clothes and get my gun. I'll pick up Obie first and then I'll swing by your house. Make sure you're ready. It gets dark early these days."

Hans and Obediah and I had looked forward to hunting after school for about a week now.

As high school juniors and good friends, we were going to try to bag some ruffed grouse in a patch of land about 6 miles from school. We'd never hunted together. Mostly, we had hunted with our dads or by ourselves and we now looked forward to our first group foray into the world of killing animals for sport.

My dad had taught me to hunt. He had a real passion for just about any kind of hunting: duck, deer, goose, grouse, pheasant, and squirrel.

As a 16-year-old, I had passed Mike Zastrow's gun safety course at Sportsmen's Park with flying colors. I'd been the second best shot in the class, second only to Dane Zenner. A real marksman in the making, my dad had told anyone who would listen. A gunner who could shoot a flea off a dog's tail. A modern-day William Tell. A chip off the old block, he had boasted.

He had given me a .410 gauge shotgun that he'd used when he was my age. That gun would bring down squirrels, rabbits, and just about any game bird.

After I got my hunting license, my dad made sure I understood gun safety. Always have your safety latch on until you are ready to fire, always point the gun away from any person you are walking with, always identify what you are shooting before you pull the trigger. From the time I got my license, every hunting outing was preceded by a litany of safety tips from my dad, who was apparently living his reincarnation as a gun safety instructor. He didn't want me to become one of those guys you heard about every year who had mistakenly shot a family member during a hunting excursion.

"I know. I know.", I always responded after his precautionary lectures. "They taught us that stuff in gun safety class. No, I'm not going to shoot anybody. What do you think, I am? A moron?"

"Well, carrying a gun is a big responsibility. I just want to remind you that you are carrying a deadly weapon and it's not a responsibility to be treated lightly."

"OK, I get the drift. Can we go hunting now. I'm not a moron."

Hunting with Hans and Obediah was a change of pace. No gun safety lectures before we began our hunt. I realized that my dad was cautioning me because he was my dad. And that's what dads were supposed to do. But after a while, the same sermon began to fall on deaf ears. After all, I was a teenager and I knew everything.

Hans and Obie and I unloaded our guns from the trunk of the '62 Chevy Impala. They'd both accused me of driving like a grandma through the cornfield, but I defended myself. "Hey, you guys can make fun of me all you want, but if I scrape off the bottom of this car in a cornfield, my parents will see to it that I never use this car again. And that will probably be the end of our hunting, unless you guys think the three of us will be able to hitch a ride out into the country when we are all carrying shotguns. So what I'm saying, boys, is maybe you should keep quiet until it's your parents' car you're riding in."

"Yeah, I suppose you're right, Symalla", said Obie, loading his shotgun. "And what are we hunting today? How about we go for some duck-billed platypus? Or is that platypii?"

"Well, let's start with something a bit more common, like maybe the ruffed grouse. Any ideas on how we should hunt this strip?"

Hans and Obediah and I surveyed the skinny stretch of brush that was in front of us. My dad and I had walked this stretch about a week before and we'd kicked up a lot of grouse. But I wasn't sure how much of that was due to our black lab. Blackie wasn't along for this trip. When I'd asked my dad if I could go hunting with my friends, he'd reluctantly agreed, but he'd nixed my request to take Blackie because he said the dog might get too excited around strangers. It might be a distraction, he said. I never pushed the idea any further, as I was just happy that he had agreed to let me go hunting with my friends.

"Well, since we don't have a dog, someone's going to have to walk through the brush and chase up the birds", I said. "Then one of us will walk the right side of the strip and one of us will walk the left side of the strip."

"Sounds like a plan", Hans agreed. "Who wants to walk the middle? Should we draw twigs?"

"I want to walk the middle", said Obie, who must have been thinking he'd get the first shot at any birds. Hans and I shared a brief look of relief, well aware that tromping through the thick underbrush would be a lot of work. Also, we knew that Obie was the biggest and clumsiest of our trio, and if anybody could scare up birds, it would be Obie.

"OK, Obie. You go down the middle", I instructed. "I'll be on the right side. Hanszel will be on the left. You shoot any of the birds which are straight in front of you on the ground. But you need to leave anything that's in the air to Hans and I. You should get first crack at everything, and then Hans and I will nail anything that flies off to the sides. And if you see that duck-billed platypus you're looking for, you might want to think twice before shooting it. I don't have my game guide with me, but I'm pretty sure they're on the endangered species list."

Obie smiled and descended into the patch of brush. It wasn't long before Hans and I heard him yell, "Holy shit. It's thick in here. I can barely tell whether I'm walking the right way."

"No shit, Sherlock. What did you think it would be like in there."

It wasn't long and the grouse were flying left and right, exploding from the patch of brush. From what I could gather, Obie would try to lift his gun to shoot, but the brush was so thick that he could never get a shot off. Obie wasn't much for swearing, but every once in a while, we'd hear a "Geez Louise" or "Gosh Darnit" coming from the brush. I smiled to myself as I pictured Obie clomping through the woods, unable to raise his shotgun because the brush was so thick.

I'd only taken one shot, not a good one, and missed. I'd quickly realized that shooting at moving targets wasn't nearly as easy as hitting the paper bullseyes in gun safety class. Most of the birds were flying left and Hans had let Obie and I know that he had already shot a couple of birds. "Got one". "Got another one". "It's like shooting carp in a barrel."

The grouse were very noisy when they went airborne and we could always tell if they were going left or right. I kept hoping that these left-handed birds would go right, but as Obie trudged through the brush, the birds mostly flew toward Hans, who was having a jolly old time.

Finally, I heard a bird heading right. I raised my gun in anticipation of the bird which would soon come into view.

Before I could get off a shot, I heard a shot from inside the brush patch. I heard the crackle of shotgun pellets as they ricocheted off brush and bushes. When some of the BBs found their way to my hip and my backside, I was suddenly able to do something I had never done before. I jumped high enough to dunk a basketball. "God dammit, Obie", I yelped like a wounded dog. "What are you doing. You just shot me in the ass."

Sure enough, some of the BBs from his 12-gauge had made his way into my derriere. "Damn that hurts", I yelled as I slumped to the ground, my life passing before my eyes.

My two hunting partners were panting as they arrived on the scene, rushing to the aid of an apparently dying companion.

When the shock of being shot had warn off, I realized that I wasn't going to die, but with two concerned friends hunched over me, I milked the episode for all it was worth. "This is it, Hans. This is it, Obie. I'm dying. Tell my family I love them. Tell Mr. Kearin that I won't be turning in tomorrow's assignment. Obie, tell my parents I said you could have my fishing gear and my shotgun. Hans, you can have first dibs at Barb Fischer. Maybe you'll have the guts to ask her out. I didn't."

"Symalla, you OK?"

"Geez, I'm really sorry. I'm sorry I hit you. Are you OK, Symalla? Do we need to go into town and call for help?"

"Symalla, I think your ass is bleeding".

Dispensing with the theatrics, discarding the martyrdom, I nevertheless continued to grit my teeth. "You're kidding me. My ass is bleeding?" Maybe I really was dying.

"Symalla, maybe we should get you to the hospital."

Jumping to my feet, I proclaimed good health and wellness. "No, I think I'll be fine. It stings like hell, but I'll be fine."

"But, Symalla, your ass is bleeding."

When I twisted my body to look down at the back of my jeans, I saw speckles of blood, but there wasn't a lot of it.

"Symalla, how bad is it? Let's see."

"Yeah, how bad is it? Let's see where you were hit. Pull down your pants."

"I'm only willing to pull down my pants for certain occasions and I can tell you right now that this isn't one of them. You pervs are going to have to get your jollies looking at someone else's ass."

The stinging had passed, but the bleeding concerned me. Hans and Obie finally convinced me to pull down my pants in the middle of a cornfield.

"It doesn't look too bad", Obie offered his diagnosis.

"Is that from a medical point of view or do you have a crush on me?", I winced.

"Looks like some BBs are stuck in your ass. Maybe we should get you to a doctor."

"No. My dad will never let me go hunting again if he finds out I got shot. My mom will never let me borrow the car again. I'll be OK. No doctor."

After much consternation, I knew that Obie and Hans were right. I should see a doctor. Hunting expedition over, we packed our guns in the trunk of the car and headed to Cold Spring. The bleeding had already stopped, but I was sore when I sat. Obie propped his hunting jacket on the driver's seat for the car ride into town. He thought it was the least he could do after he had nearly killed me.

"You know, I just got turned around in there. I couldn't tell right from left. I didn't know where I was shooting, I guess", he apologized again and again.

21

"OK. Enough already with the apologies, Obie. I know you weren't trying to kill me. Despite your concerns, I think I'm going to live. You'll see me in English class tomorrow."

On the short ride into town, we'd agreed that I'd see Doctor Carlson. He was the town doctor. He wasn't our family doctor, but I had met him when he'd done our high school sports physicals. He seemed like someone who could confirm that I was not going to die, and someone who could treat my wounds before sending me on my merry or wary way.

Most importantly, we were hoping that he could keep a secret. Hans and Obie and I had already sworn each other to secrecy. If word got around school that we had shot each other by mistake, we'd be the laughingstock of the entire school. We'd be the Three Stooges to anyone who heard the sordid details. We also knew that if any of our parents found out about our mishap, they'd surely put an end to our hunting expeditions.

The three of us sat in the empty lobby of the doctor's office while the nurse consulted with Doctor Carlson. "Geez, I hope Doctor Carlson doesn't tell my parents about this. If he does, I'll be grounded for life."

"Man, I sure hope not. If my parents find out, I'll never see the light of day again."

"You know, I think Doctor Carlson is a hunter. Maybe he'll understand. Especially if we beg him not to tell our folks."

"Thomas. Doctor Carlson will see you now", the nurse summoned me.

I explained the incident to an interested Doctor Carlson before he asked me to pull down my pants. With the high school physicals and all, it seemed like I had my pants around my ankles every time I saw him.

Doctor Carlson used a tweezers to meticulously remove over a half-dozen 12-gauge pellets from my lily white ass. The clank of each BB against the bottom of the metal bedpan reminded me of the trouble I'd be in if my parents found out that I'd been involved in a hunting accident.

"Well, son. Looks like you'll be OK. The pellets didn't penetrate far. I'm going to clean your wounds now with some disinfectant. I think this is going to sting a bit, but I have to make sure you don't get infected. Here, take this towel and bite on it if it hurts. If it hurts too much, let me know."

Thankfully, the pain was minimal.

"So, are you Matt's boy or Al's boy?", he asked.

I thought about telling him I was a stray, because I would be soon if my parents found out about this accident, but I couldn't lie.

"I'm Matt's boy", I said sheepishly, hoping Doctor Carlson wouldn't hear me, "but you won't tell him about this, will you? Whatever this visit costs, my friends and I will pay you. We'll pay the entire amount. If we don't have enough money on us, we'll give you what we have today and I'll bring you the rest tomorrow after school. No need to call my dad, Doctor Carlson. Please."

Busy taping a large patch of gauze over one of my ass cheeks, Doctor Carlson never responded.

"There we go. You're good as new, young man. I want to see you again tomorrow after school to make sure everything is OK, but other than that, you should be good to go."

He walked me out to the lobby of his office, where Hans and Obie were nervously waiting. None of us was as concerned about my condition as were were about Doctor Carlson contacting our parents.

I asked Doctor Carlson how much it had cost to pull BBs out of my ass. I had already determined that I only had $7 in my wallet. Hans and Obie were quick to reach for their wallets also.

"Well, boys, today just might be your lucky day. I think we have a special running today on pulling out BBs. There will be no charge for my services today", he said, winking at Nurse Stafford. "I'm sure you boys have already figured this out, but you need to be careful out there when you are hunting. You were lucky today. But, if there's a next time, one of you could get seriously hurt. Thomas, I'll see you tomorrow after school. I need to check for infection. And you may have trouble sitting for a while. If you do, use a pillow. Be careful, boys."

As we exited his office, it didn't seem like Doctor Carlson was going to contact our parents. Hans and Obie had remained anonymous, however Doctor Carlson and his wife lived on the same block as Hans, who later admitted that he had stolen tomatoes from Doctor Carlson's garden when Hans was young and mischievous. "I won't be stealing any more tomatoes, at least not from him and Mrs. Carlson", Hans had said.

I had remembered that Doctor Carlson and his wife Adele were members of the Ball & Chain Club with my parents. Hopefully, he wouldn't divulge the story at the monthly Ball & Chain get-together. If he did, my parents were sure to depart abruptly.

From that time on when I went hunting with my dad and he gave me the standard precautionary lecture on gun safety, I was always looking for signs as to whether Doctor Carlson had told him about my office visit. My dad's lectures remained the same. I could never see any signs that Doctor Carlson had told him about the BBs he had plucked from my ass.

Either way, after my dad's ritual lectures, I never again asked him if he thought I was a moron. After all, I knew better.

A Couple of Cookie Stories

As I recently enjoyed some of the snickerdoodles cookies which my mom had made for me, it brought to mind two of my favorite cookie stories…

A Twin Cities corporate executive told a story in which he purchased a small bag of cookies from a vendor in a Food Court at one of the local shopping malls. With his bag of cookies, this corporate executive then sat down to read his daily newspaper at one of the small tables in the Food Court dining area, which was loaded with holiday shoppers.

Soon after, a stranger (an elderly man) sat down at the table with the executive. This surprised the executive some, but when he looked around he could see that there were no other empty tables in the eating area and that explained the elderly man's presence.

The executive had yet to start to eat his bag of cookies, so he was amazed when the elderly man reached into the bag of cookies and helped himself to a cookie.

Stunned by the audacity of the elderly man, the executive didn't say anything. He decided to stay Minnesota Nice. But he also decided that he better have a cookie before his "new friend" ate them all. He reached into the same bag to have himself a cookie. The old man smiled at the executive when he did so, but never said a word.

As the executive continued to read his paper, neither of these two people had yet to say a word to each other.

Finished with his first cookie, the elderly man helped himself to a second cookie, still not saying a word to the executive. Not to be outdone, the executive took his second cookie from the bag, leaving only one cookie remaining in the bag. Now pretending to read his newspaper, the executive was interested to see if the old man had the chutzpah to help himself to the last cookie.

Sure enough, after the elderly man had finished his second cookie, he took the last cookie out of the bag, looked at the executive across the table from him and smiled as he broke the cookie in half and offered one of the halves to the executive. The executive frowned and then sighed as he reluctantly accepted the remaining half of "his" cookie.

The elderly man finished his half of the cookie, smiled at the executive, and spoke the first words between the two as he departed the table. "Have a nice day", the elderly man told the executive.

After the elderly man had left the table, the executive was still bothered by what had transpired. Also, he was disappointed that he hadn't at least told the old man what he thought of the man's bold behavior. After all, walking up to someone's table and proceeding to eat their cookies without saying a word was flat out disrespectful.

Still mumbling to himself, the executive decided to finish his shopping. When he picked up the remainder of his newspaper, he found a full bag of cookies, his cookies, resting untouched under his newspaper.

He had been helping himself to the elderly man's cookies.

A similar cookie story with a similar moral was told by someone I once knew…

Years ago, when Maggie was a first semester freshman at the University of Minnesota-Duluth, her mom would send care packages which would always include a welcome batch of homemade cookies.

In an effort to bond with a roommate she'd just met (and a roommate who seemed relatively normal), my friend Maggie would always offer some of her mom's cookies to her new roommate. The roommate would always graciously decline, saying she was on a diet.

Yet, over the course of the semester, Maggie would wake up some mornings and find that her cookie containers had been emptied. When she noticed a trail of cookie crumbs on her roommate Rebecca's desk, she had no doubts about the identity of the cookie culprit.

But when Maggie confronted Rebecca about the missing cookies, her seemingly normal roommate denied the accusations vehemently.

Other than thinking about asking her mom to send the cookies directly to her roommate, Maggie decided to let the problem ride. Maybe there was a slight possibility Rebecca was telling the truth. If not, Maggie was disappointed to think that she might be living with someone who would knowingly lie to her.

The mystery was solved in the middle of the night one night when Maggie was awakened by mysterious munching sounds. She watched in stunned silence as her roommate devoured cookie after cookie as she sat at Maggie's desk.

Finally, Maggie mustered the courage to confront her roommate. "Caught in the act, Becca!", she yelled to her roommate. "I knew it was you. And now I've caught you red-handed! Would you like me to get you some milk for those cookies?"

Without acknowledging Maggie, her roommate continued to consume the cookies.

When Maggie yelled even louder, she finally woke her roommate. Rebecca was embarrassed to find out that she had been eating Maggie's cookies during her sleep. When Maggie and Rebecca finally realized what had been happening, Rebecca joked that she now knew why her diet wasn't working. They both had a good laugh about it and agreed that future food packages from Maggie's mom would be secured under lock and key.

As these two cookie stories indicate, sometimes things aren't as they seem.

Metamorphosis

On a Saturday morning, a pile of fresh bottle caps awaited me outside the door of the dance hall. Among smells of stale beer and cigarettes from the night before, I sifted through the treasure trove. I was looking for Coca-Cola caps, the undersides of which contained the black-and-white illustrations of all the Minnesota Twins baseball players. I was determined to collect them all.

If only I could tell the dance hall bartender to be more careful when he opened the Coke bottles. There was nothing worse than discovering the Jimmy Hall cap I'd been looking for, only to find it bent in half by a reckless bartender who didn't know his work was being inspected by a 10-year old boy. If he had the time, I'd be willing to teach him the proper technique for opening a pop bottle. I'd perfected this technique as I worked toward completing my collection and it was guaranteed to leave the bottle caps completely unscathed.

After sorting through the new cache of bottle caps, I assembled my take of about a dozen and a half caps, all of which were doubles, and crammed them into the front pocket of my jeans.

Before walking home, I decided to check out the swamp in back of the dance hall. The Dance Hall Swamp sometimes provided some interesting stuff. Just a couple weeks ago, Joey Stuckel had found a ladies bra beside the swamp. As young boys, we wouldn't figure out until years later how a lady could lose her underwear in the back of the dance hall.

Once in a while, we'd see the woodchuck who lived under the dance hall. Markie Westrum had stepped in a garter snake's nest in the area surrounding the swamp.

"What was it like to step into a pit full of baby snakes?", we asked eagerly.

"Kind of like a big bowl of cold spaghetti", mused Markie.

Markie had made the biggest discovery of all when he found a young pig tangled up in an old barbwire fence on the back end of the Dance Hall Swamp. He'd come knocking on doors to gather up all the neighbor kids in the hopes that we could untangle the pig and set him free. As pigs weren't indigenous to our neighborhood, this was a big deal indeed. But when we got to the Dance Hall Swamp, Markie was the only kid who wasn't afraid to touch the poor, frightened animal, who was bleeding like a stuck pig.

When Markie finally separated the pig from the barbwire, the squealing pig ran all over the neighborhood, chased by five or six boys who wanted to help him. All the kids chasing the pig just made him more scared. Eventually, he was too tired and too hurt to run anymore and he laid down in Stuckel's yard. Officer Cheeley, the town sheriff, appeared soon to lend assistance after one of the neighbor ladies had called to tell him there was a pig on the loose. Officer Cheeley lifted the small pig into the trunk of his squad car and told us he would take it to Doc Ellis, the town vet. The pig had probably wandered from one of the area farms, he said, although the nearest farms were miles away.

Officer Cheeley thanked us for saving the pig. We later found out that the pig was in such bad condition that he ended up at the town slaughterhouse. In the immediate weeks after the young pig's demise, I had asked Mom not to make pork chops or ham for supper. I wanted to make sure we weren't enjoying the troubled friend we had hoped to rescue.

On this Saturday, as I searched the Dance Hall Swamp for things of interest, I found the swamp to be black with unidentified creatures swimming in all directions. I'd never seen fish in the swamp. It was too shallow for fish, wasn't it?

Without hesitation, I ran to my friend Wally's house to share my secret. Wally knew everything about all kinds of creatures. His dad fished and trapped all the time, and he had taught Wally about all things furry, scaly, and slimy.

"Wally, you have to come with me to the dance hall", I exclaimed, gasping for breath lost in my excitement and the two-block sprint to his house. "You have to see what I found in the swamp. There must be millions of them. They look like the big black swarms of baby bullheads we saw in the river last year, but they're not swimming in schools. They're not bullheads. You have to come and see, Wally. Get a coffee can or an ice cream bucket. We need something to catch them with to see what they are."

Wally was eager to accompany me to the dance hall. When we arrived, I showed him the hoards of black swimming creatures. He too was in awe. "Wow, look at that", he shouted. "I know what those are", immediately shedding his shoes and socks and rolling up his jeans.

"Be careful. There's probably broken whiskey bottles in there", I cautioned.

Wading into the water with an empty Maxwell House coffee can usually reserved for the grub worms we used as fishing bait, Wally scooped up some of the mysterious creatures.

"What are they, Wally? What are they?" I looked into the can, where a half-dozen creatures with bulbous eyes were clearly visible against the silver walls of the can. It was weird. Some of the creatures had tiny black legs, Some didn't. Some of the creatures had black tails. Some didn't.

Wally reached into the can and gathered one of the creatures so we could take a closer look.

"You know what these are?", he asked. "These are tadpoles. They start out as fish and then they grow legs. Won't be long and they'll be frogs. Sister Elise calls it metamorphosis or something. I call it weird.

"My dad says there will be a ton of frogs this year. Water's high and there's lots of swamps. He said there were so many frogs migrating one year that they had to close Highway 23 by the rookery. Cars were sliding into the ditch because there was so much frog gunk on the road. He said the county sent out snowplows to scrape all the slimy frog guts off the highway. That must have been something, huh?"

Wally emptied the coffee can and we headed home, agreeing that this would be a secret just between us. We'd make daily visits to the swamp to watch the tadpoles turn into frogs. Metamorphosis.

Wally and I were good friends. We were in the same grade in school and we lived only a block from each other. As grade school best buddies, Wally, Jimmy Nissman and I would walk home from school for lunch, where our stay-at-home moms would have lunch waiting for us. On these lunch respites from St. Boniface, the walk home was always much faster than the walk back to school, because we were hungry. We'd sometimes dawdle on the way back from lunch, despite warnings from our moms and the nuns at school.

We'd often stop to visit Jimmy's grandma, who was always glad to see us and who always seemed to have a fresh batch of cookies to offer us. We almost always stayed too long at Jimmy's grandma's house and we knew it. Before we left, we'd assemble a bouquet of flowers from her garden to present to Sister Susanne when we walked into a class which was already well in session.

Sister Susanne was a sucker for a good bouquet of flowers, and, although she always reprimanded us in front of the class, she didn't have the heart to yell at us full-bore. She always ended her lecture on the pitfalls of being late to class with a "but thank you for the flowers, boys. May God bless you." We knew that Sister Susanne was aware of our charade, but she never ended it , and neither did we.

The following year, when we tried to pull the same stunt with Sister Arlene, our second grade teacher, she promptly ended the practice by immediately disposing of the flowers into her metal wastebasket and threatening to shove her wooden blackboard pointer into cavities of our bodies that hadn't previously been visited. With Sister Arlene's threats, our ruse ended and so did the post-lunch visits to Jimmy Nissman's grandma.

Wally and I remained good friends throughout grade school. We were altar boy partners. We fished for sunnies, crappies, and bullheads off Zastrow's Bridge. We scoured the banks of the nearby Sauk River for painted turtles who were sunning themselves. When I got a crush on Missy Dunston in the fifth grade, Wally got a crush on her too. It didn't matter to us that we both had a crush on her. Missy didn't know that either of us was alive.

Wally and I played one-on-one baseball games in my back-yard and his driveway. We played one-on-one basketball games in my driveway. No matter how hard Wally tried, he couldn't beat me at basketball or baseball. When I finally let him win in basketball, he never played me again.

Wally was the shortest kid in our class. His eyesight wasn't very good and he wore big black plastic glasses with Coke bottle lenses. One of his legs was longer than the other because he'd apparently been hit by a car when he was a young boy and one of his legs had stopped growing for a while. With his physical shortcomings, Wally was a target for kids who liked to pick on other kids. When Brucie Baldwin, one of the younger kids at school, called Wally a "flamingo" during recess, I gave Brucie a bloody nose. No one would pick on my friend, I told a whimpering Brucie.

On the way home after school that day, Wally had cried, not because Brucie had made fun of his different-sized legs, but because I hadn't let him fight his own fight. He didn't need anyone to look out for him, he said.

Toward the end of grade school, Wally and I began to grow apart. I was never quite sure why we didn't hang around much anymore, but I was sure I missed his company.

By the time we reached high school, we barely said hi as we passed each other in the halls. Wally didn't like baseball anymore. He didn't want to sit with us in the cafeteria, even though he was always welcome. He had found some new friends, he said.

I was never sure if Wally knew how his new friends talked about him. Marshall Schoenfield and Todd Moran were quick to tell anyone that Wally was their "boy". He'd run their errands and provide cheap entertainment by accepting their dares, they said. In return, they'd offer Wally cigarettes, 3.2 beer, and occasional party invitations.

By now, Wally had made it clear that he no longer appreciated my protection or concern. He could stand up for himself, he said, and anyway, his new friends would look out for him. Unfortunately, I respected his wishes and never again stepped in to help him.

As part of freshman initiation at St. Boniface, Wally got stuck with an unusually mean Big Brother. Although these high school seniors were supposed to help their freshman counterparts get acclimated to high school life, some Big Brothers opted instead to torture their Little Brothers.

While most Big Brothers were forcing their Little Brothers to spit-shine their shoes, build the Homecoming bonfire, and do duck walks across the field during the Friday night football games, Wally was left to fend for himself. As part of high school initiation, he was dropped off at Big Fish Lake in the middle of the night and left to walk four miles back to town. On another fall evening, he was tied up and dumped in the town cemetery, forced to spend the night alone with his vivid imagination, until his Big Brother was gracious enough to finally release him the next morning.

In the summer between my sophomore and junior year, my parents received a call in the middle of the night. Even though the door to my bedroom was closed, I knew that whatever news came from a middle-of-the-night phone call couldn't be good, especially since I'd heard the siren of the town ambulance along Highway 23 only a couple of hours earlier.

The call was brief, but the conversation that followed between my parents was much longer, even though I couldn't hear what they were talking about.

It could wait until morning, I thought. I had to work at the hardware store early in the morning. I rolled over and went back to sleep.

As I slopped on jeans and a wrinkled t-shirt the next morning, my parents appeared at my bedroom door.

"What was all the commotion about last night?", I mumbled.

"Oh, we have some terrible news", my mom responded. "Wally Westrum was hit by a car last night when he was riding his bike home from a party in Rockville. The driver of the car never saw him. They rushed Wally to the hospital in the ambulance, but he died before they got him there."

Leaving my mom to tell herself about the details of the accident, I headed toward the bathroom to brush my teeth and prepare for the day of work at the hardware store.

Struck by my nonchalance, Mom was quick to question me. "Tom, did you hear what I said? Wally's dead. Wally's dead. Doesn't that bother you?"

"Mom, what am I supposed to say? How do you want me to react? If you ask me, Wally was dead to me a long time before last night. He and I weren't friends anymore."

When I arrived at work that day, Wenner's Hardware was fraught with the somber news of the night before. John and Charlie Wenner, the owners of the store, also owned the town ambulance service and the town funeral home. The daily paper from St. Cloud wouldn't be out until later that afternoon, so some of the people in town suddenly decided they needed a couple of wood screws for the project they were working on and they wandered into the hardware store in the hopes of getting some specifics about the previous night's accident on Highway 23.

My co-workers and some of the customers knew that I was a classmate, a neighbor, and a childhood friend of the boy that had died and they were quick to ask me what I knew of the previous night's events.

I knew nothing, I said without expression or interest. When I got tired of people fishing for the morbid details, I decided to retire to the back room of the store to repair broken windows and torn screens.

In a room filled with empty extra caskets from the funeral home, I laid the window screens on the linoleum floor, where I'd roll the new screens into their frames.

I thought about Wally's death. I flashed back to some of the things we'd done as kids. As I did, my lack of emotion haunted me.

Rolling a screen into its aluminum frame, I noticed the tears that began to fill the squares of the screen. I was relieved that I'd finally responded to the news from the night before. But even then, those tears weren't for the teenage boy who had died in a bike accident. They were for a friend I'd lost long before he died.

That Was Then, This is Now

Every time I drive past the baseball fields on Cleveland Avenue, I'm reminded of how things have changed from when I was a kid. Things are different now and we should all feel bad about that.

RED RIVER AVENUE, COLD SPRING, MINNESOTA. EARLY 1960's. We needed a place to play ball. A place where there were no windows to break, a place where there were no lawns or gardens to trample, and a place where there were no moving cars to get in the way of an outfielder chasing an extra base hit.

Tiny Bautch had a field in which he usually planted corn, but corn prices hadn't been very good the past couple of years and it was no longer worth Tiny's while to plant the small field at the end of our block. Mr. Vogt had talked Tiny into letting the neighborhood kids use part of the vacant corn field as a baseball field. Eagerly, we had helped Mr. Vogt lay out the new home field of the Red River Rats. It was nothing fancy. No dugouts, no backstops or fences, no scoreboard. But it became a haven for about a dozen grade school kids. It was a place where we were free to be kids, free from the more complicated world of adults.

Throughout the summers, we'd play baseball two, sometimes three, times a day. We used old wooden bats, some held together by nails and tape, to pound around baseballs that were often coming apart at the seams. Sometimes, we'd also pound around each other with occasional fisticuffs and verbal sparring matches. But any bad blood between us was always quickly forgotten when we got together to play baseball again.

We organized our own games, picked our own teams, made our own rules. If we didn't have enough players to cover the entire field, batters were required to hit to the left of second base or the right of second base, depending on whether you were a right- or left-handed hitter. Any ball hit to the wrong side of the field or any ball not hit out of the infield was an automatic out. Occasionally, when we wanted to change things up a bit, we'd have switch-hit games in which right-handed batters would have to bat left-handed and left-handed batters would have to bat right-handed.

Almost always after our games, we'd make time for Billy Steil, a neighborhood kid with down's syndrome. Billy loved baseball and he always wanted to play. He was too young to play in our regular games, but we always made sure he got his share of swings when our game had ended.

We organized our own games and there were no parents, athletic associations, or umpires to enforce the rules or mediate our disputes.

Every once in a while, one of us got hurt, usually hit in the face by a ball that had taken a bad hop on one of the old corn row humps. Whoever got hurt would cry, whine, squeal, or swear, then when he was done, he'd be ready to resume the game.

When we really wanted to have fun, we'd organize games against the kids from other areas of town. As acting manager of the Red River Rats, I'd spend hours writing down possible lineup combinations for these bragging rights games. If only I had worked as hard at my homework.

For road games against the Frogtown Froggies or the Brewery Hill Bombers, we'd all hop on our bikes and caravan our way across town to defend the honor of the Red River Rats. If we won the games against our crosstown rivals, we'd be happy to tell anyone who would listen. If we lost, there would always be another day. As important as these games were in a young boy's world, there wasn't an adult to be found at any of them.

It's been years now since those games when I was a kid. Although the memories are still vivid, I can only imagine what would happen if I was a child today...

MAIN STREET, ANYWHERE, USA. TODAY. Mr. Vogt called Tiny Bautch to see if part of his corn field could again be used as a youth baseball field.

Tiny declined the request, citing liability concerns. Apparently, the year before, one of the kids had taken a baseball to the face after it hit one of the corn row humps. The kid was OK, and despite a busted lip, continued to play because he loved playing baseball and a fat lip was not a big deal. The kid's dad, however, saw it differently, and called Mr. Bautch, threatening to sue him for everything he owned.

"You're responsible", he yelled at Mr. Bautch. "Things like this just don't happen to my kid. Somebody's got to be blamed. The bumps in the field are your fault. I don't care if you were trying to be a good guy in letting those kids use your corn field. My kid has a split lip and someone has to pay. I'll have your ass in a sling when I'm done with you."

With the corn field no longer available, the kids in the neighborhood had to go to the city park to play their games. But even though the city park was less than a mile away, the parents wouldn't let their kids ride bikes to the park…and rightfully so. Although it had been a number of years before, the memories were still fresh of the 11-year-old boy who had been abducted by a stranger in broad daylight as the boy and his two play buddies rode their bikes in a town only nine miles away. The young boy was never to be found again and his mom started a missing children's foundation in his name.

So, after being dragged away from their computers and their television sets, the kids rode in mom and dad's minivan to the city park to play their games. And the parents decided that as long as they were there, the games would be better if they were supervised by adults.

The wooden bats with nails were replaced by $100 aluminum bats. Associations were formed, umpires were hired, and coaches were appointed. The kids were outfitted in fancy uniforms supplied by corporate sponsors. The verbal sparring was still present, but it was now mostly between the parents and the umpires, the parents and the coaches, and even the parents and their kids or other parents' kids.

When there was a disagreement between the kids, there were no fisticuffs. But one of the kids involved in the disagreement mentioned to his teammate that he could get a gun and make those other kids pay.

Things are different now and we should all feel bad about that.

Regular Again

It was a Monday morning on campus. With the throbbing pain in my stomach, I hadn't been able to sleep.

"What's up with you, Tommy?", my roommate had inquired. "Man, you were moanin' and groanin' all night."

"Yeah", I grimaced. "I'm a hurtin' pup. I've got one helluva gut ache. The Mystery Meat in the cafeteria must have got the best of me."

The food in the cafeteria was OK, but there were no limits to the number of helpings. As I had adopted a quantity over quality approach, stomachaches weren't all that unusual.

"Where is your pain?"

"What, you're a doctor now? It's right here". I pointed to my lower right abdomen.

"You better go to the infirmary. My brother had a pain in his right side and it turned out to be his appendix."

"Maybe I'll go there this afternoon if it doesn't get better."

"Man, I'd go now. If it's your appendix and it bursts, you could get seriously sick. No sense pushin' up daisies before you have to. I'll see you later. I'm off to my 8:15. Go to the infirmary."

The infirmary opened at 9 a.m. I decided to get there sooner than later. My pain was almost unbearable and it wasn't getting any better.

Maggie O'Halloran was the nurse in the infirmary. Middle-aged, heavyset, and with the vocabulary of a seasoned sailor, she was a favorite of many students. An avid sports fan, she sat with us at some of the games. We were her boys and even in a crowded gym or rink, we always made room for Maggie.

"Hi, Maggie", I mumbled between gritted teeth as I entered the infirmary.

She didn't know me by name, but she remembered me from the Friday night hockey game where my buddies and I had shared our schnapps with her.

In an earlier hockey game against rival Gustavus, a skirmish had ensued between the teams' fans. It was a short encounter with few fisticuffs, but a lot of verbal sparring. Security guards had stepped in quickly to end the pushing and shoving. But surrounded by St. Thomas football players, Maggie had gotten in a couple of good licks with her wooden cane. Some of the raucous Gustie fans were bewildered as they fended off blows from a middle-aged lady with a walking stick.

When fights between jocks broke out, I was usually mysteriously absent. But I knew that if I ever got in a fight, I wanted Maggie O'Halloran on my side.

Maggie also knew me from our annual St. Pat's Day visits to the infirmary. My friends and I had always visited the infirmary first thing in the morning on St. Pat's Day, all of us claiming to be afflicted with sore throats.

With a twinkle in her eye, Maggie sprayed our throats and swore us to secrecy. This was a campus tradition that was starting to get out of hand, she said. But with a last name like

O'Halloran, she appreciated our St. Pat's Day enthusiasm, and encouraged us to enjoy the day and to "make sure to know when to put the cork in the bottle."

"Yeah, after we've finished the bottle, Maggie", we said as we were on our merry way.

Maggie O'Halloran knew very well that we didn't have sore throats when we visited. No throat cultures were prescribed. She knew that the throat spray she administered to her sick patients would allow them to urinate green throughout the day. Those of us who had been sprayed looked forward to standing next to someone at a urine trough or urinal and gleefully pointing out, "Hey, it must be St. Pat's Day. Look, my piss is green". We all got a chuckle out of our juvenile humor. Even guys who admitted to nervous bladders got sprayed by Maggie. After a few beers, even the meek were uninhibited enough to show unsuspecting whiz mates their Irish green artistry.

"Whatsa matter, honey?", Maggie asked. "You look white as a sheet."

"I got a nasty stomachache, Maggie. Is there anything you can do to help me?"

"You poor thing", she sympathized. "The doctor is in this morning. Come with me and I'll have him take a look at you."

Doctor Fox asked me a set of questions. He eventually felt my right side and I yelped like a dog who had been stepped on.

"Son, I think you have appendicitis", he said. "I'm going to have you go to the hospital immediately. I'll have them do some blood work and we'll see if your white count is high. Do you need directions to St. Joseph's? You should probably get someone to drive you there. I'll tell the hospital to expect you by 10 o'clock."

I was in too much pain to try to delay the tests. Hunched over, I walked back to my dorm in hopes of finding someone to drive me to the hospital. But it was Monday morning and everybody had classes. The dorm was empty. Doctor Fox had told me that I needed to get to the hospital immediately, so I drove myself.

Fighting tears and extreme pain, I almost passed out at the wheel. Sweating and nauseous, I stumbled into the hospital lobby and handed them the paperwork from Doctor Fox.

Tests showed that my white count was high and I indeed had appendicitis. The doctor at the hospital relayed the results of my blood test and told me that I'd need immediate surgery to remove my appendix. "Doctor Fox will do the surgery", he said. "We'll do it as soon as he gets here. He's on his way."

As the orderly escorted me to the room where they would prepare me for surgery, I remembered my only other experience as a surgery patient. Six years old, I'd had my tonsils removed. I didn't remember much about the surgery, but I remembered vividly the teenage boy in the bed next to me. He was really having a tough time of it, in a lot of pain.

As my parents sat next to my hospital bed, I was all excited because my dad had promised me a ride home in his truck. I had never had a ride in Dad's Cold Spring Beer truck and I couldn't wait to ride in the passenger seat on the 16-mile trip from the St. Cloud Hospital to Cold Spring. At the time, I was just interested in getting a ride in Dad's truck. Years later, I might have been more excited about the fact that it was a beer truck. Some of my best dreams have involved beer trucks and bikinis.

Recuperating from my tonsil surgery, I was enjoying strawberry Jell-O and Brown's ice cream while my hospital roommate was writhing in pain. With all the tubes and wires running into or out of him, it was no wonder he was in so much pain.

"What's wrong with him?", I had asked.

"Oh, his appendix burst", the nurse replied matter-of-factly. "He's in a lot of pain now, but he'll be OK."

As a wide-eyed six-year-old, I'd decided then and there that I never wanted to have my appendix taken out.

But now as I was being wheeled to a surgery prep room, that was exactly the fate that awaited me.

My parents had been listed as the people to call in the case of a medical emergency. My mom was a nurse's assistant at the high school; the hospital contacted her to inform her of the pending emergency surgery. I knew that she'd have to reach my dad, as they would both want to come and my dad would have to be the designated chauffeur, as my mom had never driven in the Cities. My dad was a traveling sales and service person and, in days before pagers and cell phones, I knew that it might not be easy for my mom to reach him. She'd have to call around to many of the grocery stores he serviced and hopefully she would be able to find him.

I later found out that my mom had requested a delay in the surgery. She needed time to locate my father and they needed to make the 75-mile drive from Cold Spring to St. Paul. Doctor Fox informed her that this would not be an option. My appendix was about to blow and the emergency surgery had already been scheduled.

I also found out later that my mom had asked Doctor Fox if he was qualified to perform the surgery. Doctor Fox assured her that he was indeed qualified, his medical license was on his office wall for all to see, my mom would be welcome to see it when she arrived in the Twin Cities, and he had to let her go as it was time to prepare for my surgery.

The prep nurse informed me that someone would soon be in to shave me. With long hair and a beard in the '70's, it never dawned on me what areas they intended to shave. Not thinking clearly, for some reason I thought they'd want to shave my beard, even though they were going to take the appendix from my lower stomach area.

I eventually realized where I'd be shaved and I was quickly uncomfortable with the thought. Things got worse when the male nurse's assistant appeared with his cart and shaving utensils.

"Symalla, is that you? Long time no see."

Pat Keegan had been a dormmate and classmate my freshman year at St. Thomas. I remembered him immediately. He was a bright, likeable guy who had spent a lot of time partying that freshman year. So I saw him a lot. Rumors were that he liked to party too much and when he didn't show up for sophomore year, I presumed that he'd either flunked out or was kicked out, quietly dismissed.

Now, as he directed a razor blade around my genitals, I hoped that he hadn't partied the night before. We discussed old times. He told me he had transferred to Macalester, a more liberal college with a political science program that suited him.

It was nice to catch up with an old acquaintance, but this wasn't my version of a reunion. On my back, with my gown pulled up, I hoped that he felt as uncomfortable as I did as he handled my manhood.

When I awoke from surgery, my parents were there. Unfortunately, the hospital short-changed me on the post-op pain medication and I awoke to more pain than I had ever had. My mind still not cleared of the anesthesia, I was quick to disperse a collection of swear words that my parents didn't know were in my repertoire. I later attributed these words to all the unsavory characters I'd met in college. My parents weren't buying it, but they were happy to find out that I had enhanced my vocabulary.

The nurse prescribed a morphine drip to ease the pain, and it did. When I regained my senses, I quickly asked my parents if they had taken out health insurance on me. I had remembered the conversation with my mom the previous summer when she had asked me if I still wanted to be included on the family health insurance plan.

"What for?", I had responded. "I'm healthy as a horse". As a 20-year-old, not only was I indestructible and immortal, I also knew everything. As someone once said about that age group, it's the only time in your life when you know everything.

I was relieved to find out that my parents had ignored my wishes and included me anyway on the family health insurance plan. It was nice to know they had finally been smarter than me, and I'd not have to spend the next 20 years working in the cafeteria dishroom at $2.15 an hour to pay for my surgery. I'd be able to return to my college classes.

The doctors informed my parents that the operation had been a success and that I should be out of the hospital in about three days. A day later, when my parents were comfortable with the idea that I would be OK, they left me to myself and drove back home to Cold Spring.

With my parents gone, I had plenty of visitors at St. Joseph's Hospital. A lot of my college friends stopped by to express their concern or to revel in the sight of me in an open-backed hospital gown. I milked my hospital stay for all it was worth. I was quick to tell visitors of my near-death experience. Yes, I had looked Death in the eye and it had run away whimpering.

I was enjoying the constant parade of visitors, including a good number of empathetic female friends from the College of St. Catherine. My affliction seemed to elevate my status with all concerned. I loved the attention and I loved not having to go to classes. All in all, my postoperative stay was turning out to be a goddamn Mardi Gras…until a couple of days after the surgery when the head nurse casually asked me if I'd had a bowel movement since the surgery.

"No, not yet", I replied. "They pay you to keep track of that?"

"Well, Thomas, if you don't have a BM by the morning, I'll schedule you for an enema. You'll have to have a BM or we won't let you go home."

She didn't need to explain what an enema was. Although I'd never had one, the thought of one scared me more than an appendectomy. The thought of a finger, hose or Roto-Rooter up my posterior made me squirm at frequent intervals.

When the night nurse introduced herself at the start of her shift, I'd already decided I needed to become regular again. She asked if there was anything I needed.

"You know, Janet, I have a sudden craving for prune juice. Would it be possible for me to get some prune juice?"

"Sure, I'll get you a carton."

"Would it be OK if I have two? I'm awfully thirsty."

"Two it is."

I'd never had prune juice before, but I'd heard about its medical benefits from Johnny Carson's monologues on "The Tonight Show". Apparently, it was the official drink of the elderly and the constipated.

When my prune juice arrived, I approached it as if it was a frosty Schmidt beer at Tiffany's Lounge and I chugged it before my taste buds had a chance to disapprove.

After drinking the prune juice, I decided that a stroll down the hall might help things along. It was just a matter of hours before I became regular again.

My Mardi Gras had ended, but I knew it was time to go back to campus again.

Innocence Lost

When the plane landed in Oakland, the flight attendant tapped a sleepy young soldier on the shoulder and said, "You had better get that uniform off as soon as you can." The young soldier didn't get a chance to ask for an explanation, as the flight attendant had moved on. He was confused by her comment. He was proud of his uniform and the service to his country that it represented. Under normal circumstances, he would have spent more time trying to figure out what she meant, but it had been a long flight and all he could think about was that he would soon set foot again on American soil. It was something he had been dreaming about. The culmination of a countdown.

The year was 1971. The young soldier had spent the past 18 months serving his country in Vietnam. There as a medic, he had tried to patch his fellow soldiers back together again. He never considered the heroics of his efforts. He was only doing his job. Sometimes his efforts were rewarded and his patients lived to see another day. Sometimes his efforts were futile and he said goodbye to soldiers who would never see home again. His job as a medic was filled with death and disability. He saw things that no young man should ever have to see.

The young soldier had a 12-hour layover in Oakland before his flight home to New Jersey. The USO was less than a mile from the Oakland airport. The weather was pleasant and he had never been to Oakland, so the young soldier decided to walk to the USO.

He had just started his walk to the USO when a car pulled up beside him and the passengers welcomed him back to America with screams of "baby killer" and "war monger". Moments later, as he neared the USO, protestors pelted him with eggs and rotten tomatoes. The young soldier hastened his pace, but not before a long-haired protestor spit in his face. The young soldier wanted to retaliate, but he restrained himself.

Safe inside the USO, the young soldier now knew what the flight attendant had been talking about. Bewildered and disappointed, he admitted to himself that he hadn't expected a ticker tape parade, but he thought he'd hear occasional thanks for doing what he and so many others had to do. His father, a World War II vet, had often told stories of the heroes' welcome which he and his fellow soldiers had experienced upon their return to the States. Obviously this wouldn't be the case for the young soldier returning from Vietnam.

The young soldier had heard rumors that he would be returning to a country in turmoil, a country divided by this war in Southeast Asia. Now, as he sat inside the USO, he realized that he didn't even recognize the country he had left. What had happened to patriotism, honor, and appreciation for those who were willing to sacrifice their lives for their country? What had happened to America?

The young soldier is a man I met at an airport bar a number of years ago. It had been almost 20 years since he served in Vietnam and it was obvious that he was still haunted by the way in which he was treated upon his return.

It was his story and he did all the talking. I was a captive audience with no immediate place to go, but I appreciated the story and expressed my understanding with knowing nods.

Eventually, I noted that my plane would be boarding soon. I shook the man's hand, wished him a safe flight, and went on to my boarding gate.

As I fastened the seatbelt in my coach class seat, I replayed the man's story in my head. His story could have been mine, I realized. After all, it was my generation.

As a high school student in a small Minnesota town, I didn't pay much attention to the war in Vietnam. It was something that was happening thousands of miles away and, most of the time, it was just another story on the 6 o'clock news.

That all changed and the Vietnam War became suddenly real for me and the other people of Cold Spring when David Weber, a local marine, returned from the war early in a flag-draped casket. His brother Fred was a classmate of mine. From that time on, the war in Vietnam wasn't just another news story about something that was happening oceans away. When the news spread around town that Gary Guggenberger, one of the kids from the next block, had been listed as a Prisoner of War, we were all interested and concerned with what was happening in Vietnam.

By the time I entered college, I knew that the military draft and a subsequent stint in Vietnam could put an end to my studies.

I'll admit that the thought of going to war terrified me. This wouldn't be like the Cowboys and Indians or Cops and Robbers which I had played with the neighborhood kids. This would be for real. The thought of having to kill other human beings frightened me. However, I also knew that if I was ever confronted by a "him or me, killed or be killed" situation, I would shoot to kill. My fear wasn't the killing itself. It was more about how it would change me forever.

As a 19-year old kid, my birth date came up 98th in the draft lottery. From the lottery in the year before, the first 95 birth dates had been called for possible induction.

By the time I entered college, I had studied the Vietnam War enough to know that it wasn't something I believed in. I wasn't one of the anti-war protestors who were featured on nightly news broadcasts. I wasn't a protestor because I was torn between serving my country and protesting a war I couldn't endorse. Both of my grandfathers had served in the Army in World War I. My father, my Uncle Al, and my Uncle Jerry had served in the Navy. Their service to our country was something I respected and admired. At the College of St. Thomas, I had friends who were part of the campus Reserve Officers' Training Corps (ROTC) program.

Fortunately for me and for all of us, the Vietnam War was winding down by the time I was included in the draft lottery. No new draft orders were issued and we finally brought our troops home. I never had to make the decision as to whether I would serve in Vietnam or seek refuge in Canada.

To this day, I still think about Vietnam, if I would have gone, what it would have been like, and how it would have changed me.

One of my customers from years ago was a retired lady who reluctantly told me that she has had to provide for her adult son who served in Vietnam.

He returned unable to take care of himself. He wasn't physically injured, she said, but he just hasn't been right ever since. When he left for Vietnam, he was a bright and engaging young man with a promising future. Now, in the care of his loving mother, he has never talked to her about his days in Vietnam. She has no idea what happened to him over there, but she knows that whatever it was, it must have been horrible.

Sometimes when I think back to all the great times I had in college, I feel a twinge of guilt. While we were toasting each other at keggers, making midnight runs to White Castle, and professing our so-called manhood by chewing the worms from the bottom of tequila bottles, there were friends we'd grown up with who were risking their lives worlds away in Vietnam.

Even for those who came back alive, their lives were changed forever. Forced to grow up much too soon, the fun and frivolity of young adulthood was no longer important.

Rick's

The Sixth Street exit off 94 took my old Jeep and I past the Metrodome, just blocks away from where I was supposed to meet my old friend Steve for a beer or two.

Steve and I had been friends for almost 15 years. Although we'd grown apart over the past three years, I was still anxious to find out what was going on in his life. Even if stories from our current lives didn't mesh, we'd have plenty of old stories to entertain ourselves for an evening.

It was Steve's invitation. He picked the place and I agreed to venture across the Mississippi River from St. Paul to Minneapolis, where we would meet at a place called Rick's.

I'd never been to Rick's, but from its name, I gathered that it was one of those neighborhood bars that I'd grown to appreciate since my move back to Minnesota. My friends Jim and Craig and I met occasionally at Nora's or Bunny's. I'd also been known to quaff a cerveza or dos with friends at watering holes with names like Billy's, Gabe's, or O'Gara's.

I liked the fact that none of these bars were like the glitz and glamour hotspots I had frequented in Dallas. Most of the bars I'd visited in St. Paul were bars where a guy with a coat and tie could sit next to a guy in steel-toed construction boots, have a beer together, and find some commonality they'd both appreciate.

So, with a name like Rick's, I hoped I'd be in for a night of peanut shells on the floor, the hovering odor of french fries and burger grease in the air, and the musty smell of stale beer coming from somewhere. For some reason, places like that always made me feel comfortable.

When I pulled into the parking lot, another old friend I saw all too infrequently got out of his car. Paul and I exchanged good-to-see-you-again handshakes. He had also been invited to Rick's.

We walked together to the entrance. I quickly noted that Rick's was Rick's Cabaret. I was a little surprised at that, but I didn't give it much thought. Gentleman's club or not, it would be good to catch up with old friends.

Steve and Rob, yet another old friend, were already seated and Paul and I quickly found their table.

We'd hardly taken a seat, when the women began converging on us like blood-thirsty mosquitoes at dusk. Four professional men in our forties, we weren't naïve enough to think these women were swarming us because they were physically attracted to us. But on what was apparently a dead night at the strip joint, we had targets on our backs.

I had heard before that size matters in strip clubs. These women were interested in one thing, the size of our wallets. They would be willing to love us for our money, as long as the money kept flowing.

Steve wore a tailored Italian suit and what was apparently a finely-crafted gold Rolex. The other three of us were dressed casually. Wearing navy Dockers and an oxford shirt embroidered with my company logo, I thought I'd be overdressed for a bar named Rick's. But I felt a bit out of place dressed as I was at Rick's, "home of the most beautiful women in the world featured daily".

Like sharks circling around their next meal, the scantily-clad women appeared in waves of two or three, introducing themselves and asking if we'd like some company. Each time, we politely rebuffed their offers, telling them we were old friends who hadn't seen each other for a while and we wanted a chance to catch up with each other first.

Paul and I had received our first drinks, Steve and Rob had received what was probably their second, when the fourth or fifth wave of strippers approached us. Steve was apparently already bored with our inner conversations. Either that or he saw something he liked, and he invited the four women to join us. If only getting a date to the prom had been this easy, I thought.

The women introduced themselves as Diamond, Chastity, Sapphire, and Rebecca. As the introductions were made, the one named Rebecca began massaging my shoulder as she stood behind me.

I'll admit that I barely acknowledged the women as they introduced themselves. I muttered a passing hello with minimal eye contact. I felt a bit guilty about being such a goddamn killjoy, but I had been excited about catching up with old friends who I didn't see often enough. We hadn't been there even 10 minutes, and we had already dispensed with the catching up part. Anyone who knows me, knows that I love the sound of my own voice and I was bound and determined to tell my old friends about my never-changing boring set of circumstances, whether they liked it or not.

"What's with this one?", the stripper who was massaging my shoulders asked my friends, referring to me. "You look like you're afraid to fly and we've just been cleared for takeoff."

I glanced at my hands, grabbing the sidearms of the comfortable cushioned armchair in which I was supposed to be relaxing. My knuckles were lily white. I would have removed my hands from the armchair, but I was afraid there would be a permanent indentation where I'd decided to prepare for takeoff. The lady massaging my shoulders was absolutely right. I was not relaxed.

What she didn't know was that I wasn't uptight because I was in a strip joint. I'd been in shaker joints before. I was uptight because I was irritated that the evening I had looked forward to had already passed.

"You look terrified", said the stripper as she finished rubbing my shoulders and slid into the last unoccupied seat at our table.

"I'm not terrified, Brandi", I said, rolling my eyes.

"My name's not Brandi. No offense intended, I just thought you were a little uptight. That's all. And by the way, my name is Rebecca."

"Yeah, yeah. Rebecca? What kind of name is that for an exotic dancer? That almost sounds like a real name. Didn't they tell you to come up with a fantasy name?"

"Rebecca is my real name", she said, proudly telling the whole table. "And these are my natural 34C breasts", sticking her thumbs on the side of her halter, as if she was about to show them off.

The synthetic conversation around the table continued without me. I was still brooding. When the conversation sectioned off, Rebecca and I were stuck to ourselves. As was her M.O., I guess, she stared at me, put her hand on my knee, leaned over and whispered her thoughts on what she'd do to me if I would just pay to go to the VIP Suite with her.

"No, I think I'll pass. I'm not much of a VIP room guy."

Working her way down the sales ladder, she then asked me if I wanted a lap dance. Into my ear, she continued to try to suck the livelihood out of my flaccid wallet as she spewed out a list of things she could do for me if I would only fork out the necessary cash. Her words made me blush. They might have made a sailor blush.

As I presume most experienced strippers are, she was a good reader of body language and she abandoned the rouse even before I had a chance to respond.

"Naw. I'm sorry, but I'm not much of a dancer, sitting or standing", I replied. She was very attractive, but I honestly hoped that she and her friends would soon head for greener pastures.

Unfortunately, for both of us, Sapphire had talked Rob into a lap dance and we continued to be stuck with each other. Fortunately, the lady named Rebecca had quickly identified that I wasn't interested in any extracurricular activities and she stepped out of her fantasy role.

"So, what do you do for a living, Tom?"

"I own a small company in St. Paul. We sell promotional items. Things like t-shirts, caps, coffee mugs, golf balls. It's a good gig. I enjoy it. Been doing it for a long time."

When we got beyond the façade, I found out that she was 33 years old, single mom of an eight-year-old son. She acknowledged that her time as an exotic entertainer was nearing an end. 33 was old for a stripper, especially in an upscale joint like Rick's.

I was no expert, I admitted, but I told her that age had been good to her, she was one of the most attractive women in the place, and I was sure that she had a few good years left before she was sent out to pasture, pardon the reference.

She didn't work Tuesday or Thursday nights, because her son played baseball those nights. Trevor was a catcher for his Little League team and he loved playing baseball.

Unknowingly, she had hit one of my soft spots. Any mom who put her son's baseball ahead of her job couldn't be all bad. She was a dedicated mom, I could tell.

She'd been stripping since she was 24, when she moved to the Cities. She'd met the father of her son before she moved to Minnesota, when she was a waitress at a Country Kitchen in Wisconsin. The first time he laid eyes on her, he announced that he intended to knock her up and marry her. She told him he was an idiot to think such a thing. Four months later, she was pregnant with his child and they married soon after. She was the idiot, she said. Her beatings started when her son was still a baby. She divorced the asshole and moved to Minnesota in hopes of a new start.

She and her son Trevor now lived in Maplewood, a St. Paul suburb. Her job as a exotic entertainer had allowed her to buy a rambler four years ago. It was a nice place for them to live, she said, and a good place for Trevor to go to school.

After she'd imparted all kinds of details about her life, she decided she'd been on the answering end of too many questions.

"Where's your office?"

"It's in the Midway District. On Transfer Road. Near the Amtrak train depot. Know where that is?"

"I think my tanning salon is near there, by the intersection of Cleveland and Marshall."

"Yeah, I know where that tanning place is. When I was in college at St. Thomas, that place was a Burger Chef. We used to eat there when we missed dinner in the cafeteria. There's a liquor store next door and a new ice cream shop across the street. Izzy's Ice Cream. Yeah, my office is about a mile from there. I drive by that salon every day on my day to work."

She and I must have talked a half-hour while the other guys in the party had gone for lap dances or were besieged by other women offering company and intimate grinding. Once Rebecca and I got past all the bullshit, my brooding and her rehearsed plastic innuendos, we had an enjoyable conversation and I decided I liked her. Not in a lap dance kind of way, but I liked her. Underneath the façade, there was a real person who I respected.

When the general manager stopped by our table to ask my friends and I if we were enjoying our evening, I caught the momentary glance of disapproval he directed at Rebecca. Clearly, it was a signal that she needed to move on and make the club some money.

I looked at Rebecca, acknowledging that I'd witnessed their non-verbal exchange.

"Looks like the bossman thinks I should move along. If it's OK with you, I'll sit here a while longer, just to piss him off."

I pulled out my wallet and extended a couple of $20 bills.

"Here, take this. Thank you for your time. I'm in a better mood now than when you first sat down. I enjoyed our conversation. It was as good as a lap dance, without all the sweating. That would be my sweating, not yours. And anyway, you probably saved me a good pair of trousers."

"No. Thanks, but I don't want it. I like to earn my money. Anyway, I was off the clock. I worked the lunch shift and bossman has already made his money off me today. I also enjoyed our conversation."

"The money's not for you. It's for your son. Will you promise to take him to a Twins game or to put it toward a new baseball bat or glove?"

"That's sweet. It's a deal."

My wallet still open, I handed her my business card. "I know you get this a lot, but maybe this is different. If you ever have some time to kill after one of your tanning sessions, stop by my office and we'll grab a bite...lunch, that is. Or call me from the tanning place and I'll take you across the street to Izzy's...that is, if you can promise to keep the whipped cream on your ice cream", I said, smiling.

She never had a chance to respond, as Rob and his escort returned from the lap dance area. I knew full-well that my conversation partner would probably toss the card in the nearest trash receptacle or tape it inside one of the men's restroom stalls. I understood the game and knew I'd never see her again, but it still felt like a good way to end the conversation.

After another beer, and continued intrusions, the night was over. As I drove home to St. Paul, I realized that through no fault of my own, I'd learned more about what was going on in a stripper's life than what was going on in my three friends' lives. That was a shame, I thought.

The following day, the events of the night before were already behind me as I sat at the front desk in the reception area of my office. I thought about where I'd grab lunch as I took a phone order from our Tony Roma's restaurant customer in McAllen.

As I was jotting down the order on a piece of scrap paper, I heard a timid knock on the front door. The door opened slowly and a dressed-down Rebecca lip-synched a "hi" as she could see I was talking on the phone.

The only person in the office, I motioned for her to have a seat in front of my desk as I finished taking the order for t-shirts, caps, and balloons. After getting all the necessary information, I thanked Leo for his order and told him his merchandise would ship that afternoon. He could expect to receive his shipment next Wednesday or Thursday in Texas.

When I hung up, I greeted my surprise visitor. "Rebecca, the grunge look suits you well." The baseball cap, the tattered jeans, and the loose-fitting sweatshirt still couldn't hide her obvious assets.

My mind ran rampant with thoughts of why she was here. Did she want a job? Did she want to go to lunch? Did she want to blackmail me? Did she want a nooner? Like I said, my mind ran rampant.

"Hi, Tom. Sorry to drop in on you like this, but I was at the tanning place and I wanted to bring you something."

She handed me an envelope. The handwriting on the envelope said, MR. SYMALLA. For Pete's sake, what had I done wrong? I finally realized that it didn't look like a summons or any other kind of legal notification. Also, I noticed that the writing on the envelope looked a bit juvenile, not like an adult would write.

Quizzical look on my face, I grabbed the scissors from the top of my paper-piled desk and slit open the top of the envelope.

"What's this?", I asked, smiling cautiously. "It's not a paternity suit, is it? Let me remind you again that you didn't give me a lap dance last night."

Unfolding the note on the yellow lined paper, I saw a carefully printed note with letters about a half-inch high.

> *Dear Mr. Symalla,*
>
> *Thank you very much for the $40. I am saving my allowences (sic) to buy a new catcher's mitt and I almost have enough to buy one. The $40 helps a lot.*
>
> *Pudge Rodriguez is my favorite baseball player. He's a catcher too.*
>
> *My mom says you are a nice man.*
> *Your friend,*
> *Trevor*

I Got the Music in Me, Somewhere

My hometown newspaper, *The Cold Spring Record*, recently printed a photograph showing all the current members of the Rocori High School Marching Band. Upon noticing the photo, I commented on how the band had shrunk over the years. In my day, if I ever had a day, the high school marching band had well over 100 members. We had numbers, and talent, to rival many college bands, we were told, and the high school trophy case could no longer hold all of the awards we'd won in various appearances around the country.

As the oldest of three kids, I wasn't sure I wanted to be part of the band. I was mostly interested in sports, and if it was an activity that didn't include throwing, catching, jumping, or tackling, I wasn't sure it was for me. But because being in the band was apparently a big deal and because all my friends were joining the band, I decided to give it a whack and see where it took me.

It all started at St. Boniface Grade School, where band first became an option in fifth grade. When I first decided to join the band, I dreamed about the instrument I'd get to play. I'd seen a new group from England called the Beatles on the Ed Sullivan Show and a couple of them were playing electric guitars. It would be cool to play an electric guitar, I thought, but I wasn't sure how my mom would take to an electric guitar, especially since she was always telling us we had to save electricity.

When Billy Kaufman told me that our elementary school band wouldn't have electric guitars, I had to reset my sights. I'd look good playing one of these shiny brass instruments, I thought. Maybe a trumpet, maybe a tuba, maybe a trombone. One of those macho instruments that was loud enough to let people know that I was in the building; something that would let people know, by decibels alone, that I was a member of the band.

I was terribly disappointed when Mr. Harris, the band director, decided that I was woodwind material and assigned me to the clarinet.

"Isn't the clarinet a girls instrument?", I balked.

"No, not at all", Mr Harris assured me. "Benny Goodman is probably the most famous clarinetist of all time and he wasn't a girl."

Mr. Harris had directed championship bands for years and I figured he had an eye for talent. Reluctantly, I figured I was meant to play the clarinet. When my parents forked out $175 for a brand new clarinet, thinking I might be the musical messiah that had been missing from generations of tone-deaf and beatless Symallas, I became a proud member of the band.

I remember the chair placements well. All the clarinet players were asked to play portions of the same musical piece unrehearsed. Then Mr. Harris placed us in chairs according to his assessment of our performance.

Although Mr. Harris had assured us that each chair was an equally important part of the clarinet section, I never believed him.

I never did well in chair placement competition. I justified my low-grade performances on the fact that I'd much rather be playing baseball than playing the clarinet. But now as an adult, I realize that I was totally void of any musical talent. To this day, I can't understand why Mr. Harris never reprehended me for the myriad of squeaks emanating from my clarinet. "Mr. Symalla, is there a mouse in your pocket or are you just happy to be here?"

Inevitably, these annual chair placements would find me near the back of the concert band clarinet section. Never last, but always a couple of chairs from being the caboose.

Fortunately for me, if we didn't agree with our chair placement, we were allowed to challenge the person seated in front of us. It was a dual of sorts, but with band instruments as the designated weapons. The winner of the challenge would get to sit in the higher chair. Unlike the unrehearsed chair placements, in challenges the challenger was able to select the tune of his or her choice…and the person being challenged had to play the same tune. Whomever played the tune better, at least in the able ears of Mr. Harris, would then receive the better chair placement. A person could do as many challenges as he wanted, however he could only challenge the person in the chair immediately in front of him.

As 11th chair out of 13, I was relegated to obscurity. I'd be seated in the third and last row of the concert band. As short as

I was, I'd be seated so far back for our annual concert that my parents would never be able to see the fancy new horn they'd bought for me.

Desperate measures for desperate times, I set out on a mission to get to the front row of the clarinet section.

I decided that "Hail to the Victors!", the University of Michigan fight song, would be my song. I practiced it day and night. To this day, my mom has unpleasant memories every time she hears the Michigan fight song played after Michigan touchdowns or field goals, usually about six to 10 times per game every time they trample our beloved University of Minnesota Gophers football team.

Practice makes perfect and I mastered this song. Not only did I get rid of all the squeaks, I was probably the only kid in fifth and sixth grade band who had memorized his challenge song. This was both impressive and intimidating to my unsuspecting victims. Within a matter of weeks, I won challenge after challenge, moving up chair by chair, never there long enough to introduce myself to the person whose chair I intended to take next.

When I finally reached second chair, I could look over my shoulder and see all the clarinetists I'd left in my trail. From second chair, only first chair Mary Arnold remained between me and the ultimate bragging right of being the best clarinet player in the band. Mary Arnold was a very good clarinet player. She'd already been in a number of state music contests playing a number of different instruments. If I could take her chair, I'd be in line for some solos during the upcoming concert.

If I did a solo, everyone would be certain to know that I was indeed an important member of the band. But if the solo involved any song other than "Hail to the Victors!", I realized that I'd be exposed as the musical fraud I really was.

I decided that second chair would suit me fine.

My band career finally bottomed out between my freshman and sophomore years of high school. My buddies had assured me that being part of the St. Boniface High School Marching Band would be a surefire way to get to spend time around our female counterparts.

At the time, the thought of getting to spend time around Mary Jo Wortz seemed like it would be good enough reason to be in the marching band. But as I soon found out, I would spend my summer as the designated lackey for Ann Schermeier.

A senior, Ann Schermeier was my row captain. She was the person who marched at the right end of the row, an honor bestowed only upon veteran band members. Everyone in our row was supposed to keep in line with her highness as we marched in step. Ann Schemeier reminded me of the marine drill sergeant in *"Gomer Pyle, USMC"*, one of the television shows my sisters and I watched. She was the spitting image of Sergeant Carter as she barked out instructions to her linemates. And she had a crew cut to match.

Ann Schermeier was my Sergeant Carter. Unfortunately, I was her Gomer Pyle. She'd taken it upon herself to make my life miserable that summer, at least until I decided to keep in line and stay in step. When I had the courage, which wasn't often, I'd reply to her orders with an elongated, "Golly". I'm not sure she ever got the Gomer Pyle inference. Either that or she didn't care. Whatever the reason, she never saw the humor in my witty retorts and she threatened to beat the stuffing out of me in front of all my friends if I didn't follow her orders.

Taking her position as row captain very seriously, Ann Schermeier was bound and determined to do her part in continuing the band's championship tradition. Me? I never saw the importance of marching in step or staying in line.

Soon after we had started practicing that summer, Ann Schermeier decided that instead of being in the middle of the row, I would march directly beside her, where she could keep an eye on me and make sure I was towing the line. I found it difficult to play my clarinet with my lips firmly implanted on her ass, but I made it work.

"Symalla, you're going to march right next to me. And you'll stay in line, won't you, honey? If you screw up during the Aquatennial parade, I'm going to kick the living crap out of you. Understand?"

"Golly", I mumbled to myself, making sure she didn't hear me, thinking of the body cavities into which she could shove my clarinet.

The Minneapolis Aquatennial was the largest parade in the state. Only the best bands from Minnesota and other states were invited to participate. Our St. Boniface High School Marching Band had won the high school division a number of times in previous years, so we were invited to again showcase our musical marching talents. The parade was such a whoopdedo that it was broadcast statewide by one of the Twin Cities' TV stations.

That Saturday afternoon in July was ridiculously hot and humid. My band uniform was soaked with sweat even before the parade started.

As we prepared to march, Ann Schermeier again made sure I understood the importance of staying in line and in step. "Symalla, remember…Left, right. Left, right, left. Step out of line even one time and I'm going to knock you on your ass in front of a statewide audience. Understand?"

"Golly. Don't worry about me, Sarge", confident she wouldn't knock me on my keister before the parade started.

Preoccupied by the thought of being pummeled by my row captain, I stayed in line and in step. But it was so hot and so humid that it was hard to play my clarinet as sweat streamed down from under my feathered hat. The salt from the sweat tasted terrible. My band uniform seemed to weigh more with every step in the 96-degreee summer heat.

While I was concentrating on whether to step with my left or my right foot, I noticed that Ann Schermeier appeared to be a bit wobbly. We were supposed to keep step with her? Walking like a drunk down main street, she was doing a lot of weaving. As I looked over to her with a what's-up-with-that look, her face went blank and she dropped to the ground like a fat sack of potatoes. Even before she hit the ground, she was out like a light.

I thought about helping her, but it all happened so fast, and, after all, she had given me specific instructions not to break my stride under any circumstances. I continued to march. Subsequent rows of captains had to step over my row captain as we continued on the parade route past the judges' stand. Within minutes, paramedics had hoisted Ann Schermeier on to a gurney and took her to an observation area as an apparent victim of dehydration and heat stroke.

As we continued along the parade route, I decided that our row looked funny without a row captain. I gradually edged my way toward the end of the row, where I became a self-anointed row captain. That day, as the only freshman row captain in the St. Boniface High School Marching Band, I ably kept our row in step and the proper distance behind the row in front of us.

After the parade, when Mr. Harris and the seniors (without Ann Schermeier) accepted our trophy, I knew I'd done my part to bring it home.

And I knew that my days as Ann Schermeier's whipping boy were over.

Arling Brinck

Running business errands late on a Friday afternoon, I'd stopped by Arling's shop to pick up the freshly printed batch of Tony Roma's t-shirts I intended to pack and ship over the weekend.

As Arling helped me load the boxes of t-shirts in my Jeep, I encouraged him to enjoy the weekend. He said he'd opted not to accompany his Shriner friends for the annual fishing opener. He'd recently lost a kidney and acknowledged the fact that he could no longer keep up with many of his fun-loving buddies. Unlike many times when I had visited his shop, we didn't talk long. I'd had a grinding week and I was anxious to put an end to it; Arling was working overtime to print a rush order and he still had a couple hours of work in front of him.

As I drove away from Arling's shop in St. Paul's Midway District, I had the same thought I'd had many times before. One of the best things about what I did for a living was the friendships I had established with some of my customers and suppliers. In some instances, including my relationship with Arling Brinck, personal friendships became much more important than business relationships. The fact that our small companies did business together was just another reason for Arling and I to keep in touch.

One of the things I liked most about Arling was that he was always trying to "build a better mousetrap". He was a creative man full of dreams and ideas. He had named his company Grand Ideas; there couldn't have been a more appropriate name.

Arling was always excited about something. Every time I walked into his shop he seemed to be excited about something new. Depending on the day, he'd tell me about the new t-shirt dryer he bought, the wooden nickel printing machine he had purchased for almost nothing at a local auction, his new button-capping machine, or his new foam beverage holder printing machine.

For those of you not familiar with the above equipment, I'll point out that these were not major purchases. They were modest purchases in a modest man's empire.

Arling and I had been friends for years. In all those years, we never discussed our personal finances. I often got the feeling that I was more financially fortunate, but I always admired Arling's zest for life. He worked hard and he loved his work. He seemed to enjoy just about everything he did, work or not.

I had met Arling Brinck soon after I started my company in Dallas. I had a number of clients in my home state of Minnesota and I was in the market for a screen printer. As our businesses were located in different areas of the country, I didn't meet Arling until I'd been doing business with him for over a year. Upon meeting him on one of my visits to the Twin Cities, we quickly became good friends.

We became each other's sounding boards for our small business endeavors. When he and his fiance' Arlene visited Dallas for an imprinted sportswear show, they stayed at my condominium. When he traveled to New Orleans for another sportswear show, I joined him there for a couple of evenings of carousing.

On his visit to Dallas, I invited Arling and Arlene to dinner at my favorite Mexican restaurant, where he and I both contacted a wicked bout of food poisoning, courtesy of some bad guacamole.

"So that's your favorite restaurant, Symalla?", he quipped after we'd both spent most of the weekend on separate commodes. "Next time I visit, maybe you can take me to one of your less favorite restaurants. If this was the best you have to offer, I can't wait to see the other restaurants you recommend."

Just about a year later, when Arling told me he was traveling to New Orleans to check out a new piece of printing equipment, we agreed that I'd fly from Dallas and we'd paint the Big Easy. After attending the trade show, we spent a night of gallivanting and rabblerousing in the Jackson Square district before we enjoyed a rare breakfast of beer, oysters-on-the-half-shell, and fried alligator in the wee hours of the morning. With lots of laughs and liquids, we agreed that this was as good as it gets.

On another of Arling's visits to Dallas, I was anxious to share my favorite watering hole and feeding trough. Humperdink, Hornblower & Witts was a Greenville Avenue establishment where the waitresses knew my name, my ale of choice, and my propensity to leave formidable tips.

After a primer of beers in the bar area, Arling and I retreated to a table for dinner in the restaurant area of Hump's.

When I order food in a restaurant, I like to make it as simple as possible, for me and for the waiter or waitress. "Yeah, I'll have the chicken fried steak with the dirty mashed potatoes, please."

Before Arling ordered anything, a long interchange between him and the waiter or waitress was always part of the regimen. "Are the Buffalo wings marinated or do you slap Tabasco sauce on them after they've been cooked? Is the fish flown in fresh or is it frozen? If I order the baby back ribs, can I get the sauce on the side? What was the name of the baby pig who donated the ribs?"

There were times when I wished that the server would have turned in my dinner order immediately after I'd ordered and before Arling ordered. There were times when I thought I could have received my order by the time Arling had finished conducting his question-and-answer period and placed his order.

On our trip to Humperdink's that night, Arling had opted for the prime rib, a specialty of the house.

I'd had the prime rib at Hump's multiple times and I'd become aware that this entrée was often accessorized with a small ceramic container of raw horseradish. As a Humperdink's newbie, Arling was unaware of this embellishment. So when the waitress delivered his prime rib dinner, Arling was quick to tell me about his disappointment in the miniscule size of the bowl of cole slaw which had been provided. "I guess I was wrong. I thought everything in Texas was big", he said. "I can probably eat the entire serving in one forkful", he complained as he picked up just about the entire bowl of horseradish with one scoop of his fork.

I knew what he was in for, but I decided not to warn him. As the large dollop of horseradish disappeared into Arling's mouth, I anticipated his reaction.

As his eyes opened wide and his nostrils flared like a bull of the Pampas, he quickly grabbed our pitcher of beer. Never bothering to transfer the beer to his glass, Arling drank directly from the pitcher.

"Damn. That's not cole slaw", he proclaimed, grabbing for more napkins to wipe the tears which were flowing from his eyes. "That's not cole slaw."

Laughing hysterically, I too had to grab for extra napkins to soak up wayward tears.

We were both still laughing when we ordered another pitcher of beer.

Back in St. Paul the Saturday after I'd picked up the Tony Roma's t-shirts, I half-listened to the radio as I was writing up some orders I had received the day before. The familiar voice of WCCO's Bruce Hagevik reported that a St. Paul t-shirt shop owner had been murdered the night before in his shop. Found dead by his fiance', 51-year-old Arling Brinck had been stabbed multiple times inside his small t-shirt shop on University Avenue.

I couldn't believe what I had just heard. Jarred from my Saturday morning doldrums, I stared silently ahead for what seemed like hours. I finally gathered myself enough to call the radio station to confirm what I had heard on their 10 a.m. newscast. They confirmed my worst fears and I sat silent again.

Arling's shop was less than two miles from my office. I went to my car and drove to his shop. The printed yellow tape across the entrance to his shop confirmed the crime. The police had already come and gone, as there were no squad cars in sight and there was no activity in the shop. After driving past his shop three times, front and alley, I resigned myself to the idea that the radio report was true.

Back in my office I called the St. Paul homicide unit to see what I could find out about my murdered friend.

"I don't know if this will help you establish a timeline, but I last saw him at about a quarter to six when I picked up some t-shirts he printed for me."

"Well, thanks for your concern, Mr. Symalla. We have some-one who talked to him after you left and we already have a suspect in mind for the crime. Unfortunately, I can't give you any additional information, as this is an on-going investigation. I'm sure you understand. But thank you for calling. I'm sorry for the loss of your friend."

I'm sorry for the loss of your friend.

The next day, the St. Paul Pioneer Press reported that Arling Brinck was the victim of an apparent robbery attempt. Stabbed multiple times in his t-shirt shop. The article pointed out that his homicide was only the third in St. Paul compared with six at the same time the year before. This was a hollow consolation, I thought, when one of the victims was one of my best friends.

Arling's small business closed immediately after his brutal murder. His two employees were left without work. His fiance' was left without a partner. His friends were left without understanding.

A recently released inmate was apprehended, eventually agreeing to a 40-year sentence. Arling's murder hadn't been the first committed by Clarence Farr. Just 10 years earlier, Farr had stabbed and brutally murdered a 58-year-old St. Paul woman in her apartment as part of a $200 robbery. He received a nine-year sentence and served almost seven before he was out to murder again. He murdered Arling Brinck for less than $50.

Less than $50? 50 damn dollars? I lost my friend so someone could have $50? How much is a life worth, anyway? It's got to be worth more than 50 bucks.

The first couple weeks after it happened, I would drive by Arling's shop just about every day, always hoping to see him emerge from his shop to give me the thumbs-up sign or to help a customer load or unload a shipment of t-shirts.

It's now been years since I lost my friend. I don't drive by his shop much anymore; I don't think about him as much anymore. But I still miss him.

Pass the Peanut Butter, Please

On a summer afternoon, he had first made himself known when I heard him gnawing on the walls of my office. I wasn't sure if he was trying to gain entrance or simply sharpening his teeth, but I quickly grabbed the Tony Roma's umbrella that was in my office and pounded on the wall, letting him know that he wasn't welcome. I didn't hear from him again that day, but I knew he'd be back.

I'd seen the red squirrels bounding and bouncing among the trees that surrounded my office. Didn't see many red squirrels in the city, I noted. They were a nice change of pace from the grey squirrels that had become plentiful and comfortable inhabitants in most St. Paul neighborhoods.

Squirrels and I had been adversaries in my teenage hunting years, but since I'd decided that I didn't like killing animals, we'd co-existed just fine. I even found them mildly entertaining, as long as they weren't gorging themselves in family birdfeeders or trying to gnaw through the walls of my office.

If a squirrel chewed his way into my office, it would wreak havoc. If I thought my office was messy now, wait until it became the site of a turf war between me and a determined gang of squirrels.

My friend and co-worker Denise had told me the story of a misguided squirrel who had made his way down the chimney and into the family living room. It turned her house into a war zone before her husband Ronnie eventually evicted it. I had just heard a story on the radio from a man who had been trying to get rid of squirrels in his attic for almost two years now.

With my office partially underground, even the pest control people might have a tough time locating the point of entry. I'd have to do something immediately, I decided, as I drove to the big box hardware store in the Midway area. In the unwanted critters section of Menards, I weighed my options. The surest way to get him would be to use a snap trap, but I didn't have the heart to be executioner for an unsuspecting squirrel.

I settled on Critter Ridder, a spray designed to repel various varmints by odor and taste. A whiff of Critter Ridder and I'd be able to bid adieu to my wannabe office mate.

I doused the area outside my office with the miracle spray. Within a week, my furry foe had decided that the scent didn't bother him at all and he was again chewing away inside my office wall. When I noticed him dabbing the spray on his puffy cheeks as if it was an aftershave, I decided it was time for Plan B.

Off to Menards, where I quickly spotted the Havahart live trap designed for squirrels, rabbits, mink, and other such creatures. This should do it, I told myself, as I plunked down my $32 for the trap. The little red fur ball would now be participating in my Critter Relocation Program, kind of like the FBI's Witness Protection Program.

Back at my office, I baited the wire trap, placing a glob of peanut butter on a strip of cardboard inside the trap. I was a bit surprised as to why I was feeding my buck-toothed buddy premium peanut butter while I had left the generic brand at home, but this would be his last meal on this premises, I thought, and he deserved premium peanut butter before I deported him.

The next morning when I checked the trap, the door was still open and my bushy-tailed adversary had licked the cardboard clean. He was indeed a member of the Clean Plate Club. There was no thank you note in sight. That ungrateful freeloader.

The following night, I placed another ample helping of peanut butter inside the opening of an empty soda can. I'd make him work for his dinner this time, and by the time he was done rummaging around with the soda can, the door of the trap would snap shut and he'd be headed for different pastures.

The next morning, I quickly noticed the orange soda can outside the trap. The trap, of course, was empty. Not only did this rodent like late-night snacks, he was a litterbug.

This time, I filled the soda can with small rocks before topping it off with a dose of peanut butter. If he wanted to carry the can out of the trap this time, he'd better be a member at Gold's Gym.

The following morning, I found the soda can drained of all peanut butter, laying as I had left it, in an empty trap.

This went on a week before I figured out that the squirrel was a lot smarter than I was. With a brain the size of a Spanish peanut, he had overmatched me. Befuddled, I called the trap manufacturer. "Hey, what's going on here? I'm trying to catch a red squirrel and he's kicking my ass. Any ideas?"

The people from Havahart informed me that I was using a grey squirrel trap. I needed to be using a red squirrel trap instead.

"I didn't realize your traps were color sensitive", I said, before they informed me that they had a different trap for red squirrels because red squirrels only weighed a couple of ounces and they weren't heavy enough to set off the trap I was using.

Off to Menards , where I plopped down another $32 for the smaller trap. How much money am I going to spend to catch a squirrel, I asked myself. The game was getting old and my wallet was getting thin. I was now reviewing the Sunday Cub Foods ads to see if peanut butter was on sale.

When I arrived at my office the next morning, I could see the small red furball inside the closed cage. Rolled up into the fetal position, he knew he'd been caught. Game. Set. Match. His premium peanut butter days were over.

Hurrying down to my office, I used the internet to see if it had any tips on how far I should transport my victim. The sites I visited told me that I'd need to relocate him at least four to seven miles away. Any shorter distance and he might find his way back.

Where would I take him? My sisters had a backyard dominated by a massive black walnut tree. Over a hundred years old, it was a haven and a heaven for lots of squirrels. Barb and Joan were both working and they might not mind another backyard inhabitant, but they only lived a couple of miles away. And what would their neighbors do if they saw me unloading a felonious rodent.

I thought about dumping him in Crosby Park, a wooded area alongside the Mississippi River. But that area was only about three and a half miles away and if I used this as a dump site, I half-expected to return to my office to find the squirrel sitting at my desk, munching on a peanut butter sandwich and sipping orange soda.

Finally, I decided to do what any self-proclaimed St. Paulite would do. I decided to dump him in Minneapolis. Fort Snelling was about five miles away. My bright-eyed and bushy-tailed captive would love it there. He'd have plenty of room to roam and plenty of trees with which to homestead. And, if he ever got homesick, he'd have to either swim the Mighty Mississippi or traipse the 494 Freeway to make it back to my office.

Hopefully, he'd like his new domicile, because if he didn't, I doubted he'd ever make it back alive. And if he did make it back, he'd deserve a hero's welcome. He and I would share an office and we'd eat Reese's Peanut Butter Cups and Fisher's Mixed Nuts for lunch every day. If he knew anything about computers, I'd anoint him as our company IT manager.

The internet article had instructed me to place a blanket over the cage when transporting the squirrel. At first, I thought this might be so the squirrel didn't know where I was taking him. Maybe I should make some miniature blindfolds. But as I read on, I found out that it was to reduce nervousness of the animal. Certainly, I didn't want to have my captive commit hari-kari on the way to his new digs. And the less of a ruckus he created, the better.

I didn't have a blanket, but I had a large box which would hold the cage. Just to be safe, I sealed the box with a strip of shipping tape. This was a smart squirrel, and if he figured out how to unlock the trap door, all hell would break loose. If I had been worried about a squirrel loose in my office, a squirrel loose inside my car while I was driving would be much worse. I already knew he had a craving for nuts and I didn't want them to be mine.

I thought about the nauseating Jeep TV commercial in which a squirrel is standing up on the passenger seat and singing "Rock Me Gently" with the car's driver. I doubted that my passenger would be receptive toward the idea of accompanying me to Aerosmith's "Dude (Looks Like A Lady)".

In my car, I zigzagged my way through my office neighborhood. I wasn't sure if squirrels had built-in GPS systems and I had seen this technique used by kidnappers in some of my favorite TV shows. I wanted to make sure he wouldn't find his way back to my office.

As I drove around the grounds of Fort Snelling, I looked for a spot to release my captive. I had planned to let him loose by the old army barracks, but that area was swarming with elementary school kids on a field trip of some kind. They'd be sure to notice the weird man with the cage and security guards would probably escort me off the property. I wasn't sure if it was legal to transport rodents across city lines.

After driving around for about 10 minutes, I finally determined the perfect spot for my furry foe. An area near the chapel would suit him just fine.

Parking my car in the empty parking lot, I opened my tailgate and used my case cutter to cut the seal of the box that held the trap.

Just months earlier, my sister Barb had told me the story of a girl who had come into the children's hospital with a squirrel's tooth embedded in her finger. Apparently, she had been feeding the squirrels somewhere, when one of them had become frightened and bit her.

I also remembered a movie in which a squirrel had jumped up to permanently become part of a character's face. What was the name of that movie? Who was the guy with the squirrel stuck on his face? Was it Chevy Chase?

I cautioned myself to be careful in releasing the red-coated rodent, who had remained remarkably calm throughout the entire ordeal. I'd make sure I was in back of the trap when I opened the door. I didn't want to drive back to the office with a squirrel attached to one of my appendages.

As I raised the door of the trap with a twig, my captive wasted no time in exiting to freedom. Only 15 yards away, he stopped to scavenge for acorns from a nearby oak tree.

I assessed the cost of the capture:

$15.95   Critter spray
$32.95   Grey squirrel trap
$32.95   Red squirrel trap
$ 3.29   Premium peanut butter
Critter Relocation: Priceless!

A Piece of Cake

When I recently inhaled a serving of my mom's strawberry shortcake, I thought back to a day when she was called into the Principal's office at Rocori High School.

Mom worked at the school in the nurse's office, across the hall from the administrative offices. The wayward ways of my sister Barb and a flying cake were responsible for Mom's meeting with the Principal.

As Symalla legend has it, Barb was suffering through an obligatory Home Economics course. The class of sophomores was learning how to bake cakes. They had split up into groups and each group had to bake their own cake, which they would then be graded on.

The cake that Barb and her small group made was a colossal flop. Instead of the moist, fluffy cake they had hoped for, their cake was hard as a rock. The geology class down the hall could have chipped away at it for hours.

Disappointed in the result of their cake-baking efforts, Barb and the other three girls in her group decided to dispose of the cake. The third floor windows were open to cool off a classroom of hot ovens. Barb and her fellow Betty Crockers decided to chuck the cake out one of the windows.

This way they'd be able to tell the teacher they hadn't made a cake and, without the evidence of a failed cake, maybe the teacher would let them make another one.

This sounded like a good plan to Barb and her compadres. It was better than getting a bad grade for the bad cake they had made. They decided it was a chance worth taking.

The best laid plans of mice and young women. They hadn't figured on Mr. Markstrom, one of the teachers, passing below the window when the cake landed on the concrete sidewalk. There's still some question as to whether the sidewalk was cracked by the crashing cake, but days later, crows were seen picking at the stones in the sidewalk while the cake nearby was left untouched. Even the crows wanted no part of my sister's cake.

After surviving this near-death experience, Mr. Markstrom promptly reported the incident of the unidentifiable flying object to the Principal. At first Mr. Markstrom thought it was a meteorite, he told the Principal, but whatever it was had a lot more density than a meteorite. Whatever it was, it could have killed him, Mr. Markstrom said. Soon after this incident was relayed to the Principal, the so-called cake hit the so-called wall and some people were in deep do-do.

The Home Ec teacher was consulted immediately and she quickly pinpointed the culprits. Barb's only salvation in this entire matter was that one of her co-conspirators was the Superintendent's daughter. The Superintendent was the Principal's boss, and that would be helpful to Barb and her partners in crime when discipline was doled out for this transgression.

Even as an adult, my mom knew that being called to the Principal's office was not a good thing. She had been summoned only once before, when our golden lab Beaver had escaped from the confines of his kennel and boarded the morning school bus. Beaver loved the kids; the kids loved him too. But when he arrived at school, he ignored the "no running in the halls" rule and created quite a stir.

One of the school's maintenance men was finally able to corral the excited labrador and read the I.D. on his collar. The maintenance man turned the problem and the dog over to the Principal, who immediately called for my mom. Mom reluctantly claimed the family dog, who seemed to be more enthusiastic about attending school than any of her three kids.

Mom may have been embarrassed by Beaver's presence at school, but she was very proud of him when he was offered a spot on the cross country team. As expected, Mom didn't express the same enthusiasm for her oldest daughter after the cake-tossing incident.

"Barbara Jean Symalla", my mom yelled as she got home from work that day. Being addressed by her full name was not a good sign for Barb that day or any day. Mom was furious. She was from a long line of good dessert makers and she promptly informed Barb that it would be a cold day in Cold Spring before one of her daughters received a bad grade for not being able to bake a cake.

Well, it was a cold day in Cold Spring when the next report cards came out and Barb received a D.

Mom's wrath was only temporary however, and Barb was eventually allowed out of the house... just in time to leave for college three years later. After the cake-tossing incident, Mr. Markstrom starting wearing a yellow hard hat as he walked the school grounds. No one is really sure what happened to the cake, but we suspect it's being used as a headstone somewhere in the town cemetery.

Fantasy, Meet Reality

It wasn't even 10 a.m. and I wanted a beer. I'd spent the past two hours trying to extinguish fires created by suppliers who apparently didn't understand the meaning of the word deadline.

"Sharon, you said you needed three weeks to produce the order", I calmly reminded our awards supplier. "We got the order to you in plenty of time and you assured us that everything was fine. Now it's two days before you're supposed to ship and you're telling me that you might not be able to make delivery? My client has a convention which starts in Lake Tahoe on the 22nd and we need to get them their awards by the 21st. Sharon, are you there?

"Sharon, you've got to get with your production department and find a way to make this happen. It's too late for me to move this order to another supplier. We're two days and counting. If you had told me that you anticipated production problems three weeks ago when I placed the order, I could have made arrangements with another supplier, but it's too late for that now. Can you call me as soon as you hear back from production? Please get with whomever you need to in order to get these awards shipped in time. This is one of my favorite clients and I don't want to let them down. Sharon, we've been a very loyal customer of your company. I hope we can continue to be a customer. Sharon, I appreciate your help. Get back to me as soon as you have any new information. Thanks."

Could the young day get any worse? Supplier problems were jeopardizing an important order with one of my restaurant chain accounts. I was scheduled to attend the franchise convention, where we'd be one of the exhibitors at the vendor expo. If I didn't get the convention awards to the client in time, I could only imagine how I'd be introduced. "Oh, and this is Tom from Promotions, inc. He's the guy who dropped the ball on our awards this year. Say hello to him now, because you won't be seeing the poor sap at any of our future conventions. We'll be calling his competitors as soon as we return from Tahoe."

As I sat alone in my office, I contemplated my misfortune by reciting a litany of swear words that would have made a swashbuckler proud. When the office phone rang again, I was sure that the day's dilemmas would mount. After all, I'm on a roll, I told myself.

My assistant Pam answered the call and then buzzed me on the intercom. "Tom, it's Sandi from the Premier Club. She says it's time for your weekly checkup. Do you want to talk to her? I told her you were in your office practicing your swear words and she says she's willing to lend an ear and make sure you are pronouncing them right."

"Sure, I'll talk to Sandi. Put her through", I said with a reluctant smile. I looked at the Mickey Mouse watch I had purchased on my recent trip to Orlando. 9:45 a.m. Sandi was like a Swiss watch. She never missed a beat.

Of all things on a morning like this, I was going to let this lady try to sell me a health club membership. No, I wouldn't take calls from any of the sales reps who were trying to get me to buy their promotional product lines, but Sandi from the Premier Club was always patched through immediately.

We'd been talking for weeks now. Once a week, every week, between 9:30 and 10 a.m. I'd been a regular guest at the Premier Club for 6 a.m. racquetball matches with my friend Charlie. We played two, sometimes three times a week when we were both in town. Sandi, the supersaleswoman that she was, had perused the guest registers for the names and phone numbers of possible prospects.

From the first day that she called, the conversation was electric. Plain and simple, Sandi gave great phone. She was magical. In her weekly attempts to get me to become a dues-paying member of the Premier Club, we broached a full menu of topics, including our weekend activities, recent movies, favorite restaurants, and pet peeves.

When we started our weekly conversation, Sandi always let me know when I had last visited the Premier Club.

"Sandi, it almost sounds like you're stalking me."

She assured me she was and then proceeded to tell me about the cooking class which she and one of her girlfriends were taking.

Always, after about a half-hour conversation, she'd ask, "So, are you ready yet?"

"No, I'm still not ready to join the club, Sandi."

"Well, OK then, Mr. Symalla. I'll call you again next week. Same time, same place. Be there or be square."

"Oh, I suppose. Have a nice week."

When I hung up the phone after talking to Sandi, I always felt better. She was better than beer, I decided. I relished our conversations and I think she enjoyed them also. Her persistence, her enthusiasm, her wit, and her moxie often made my day.

What Sandi didn't know was that I'd already decided to join the Premier Club. The guest fees from playing there as frequently as I was were killing me and the guest registration process was lengthy, especially at 6 in the morning. Einstein that I was, I'd figured out that it would be cheaper for me to become a member.

Even after I'd decided to join the Club, I decided to prolong the weekly courtship process, because I enjoyed it so much.

What would I do if Sandi grew weary of the wooing process? If she ever missed her weekly Wednesday call, I knew it would be all I could do not to call her to make sure she was OK, or to make sure she hadn't given up.

During one of our conversations, I finally surmised, as I had hoped, that Sandi was single. Fuel to the fire, I wasn't sure if she was dating anyone. She talked mostly about going out with girlfriends. I had no idea how old she was, but when I mentioned that we were doing a project for AARP, she thought AARP was the sound that a seal makes, so I figured we were similar in age.

I'll admit that I often wondered what Sandi looked like. With a golden personality like hers, she couldn't be attractive, the glass half-empty side of my constitution cautioned me. I was always in and out of the Premier Club by 7:30 after my racquetball matches with Charlie. Soon after we started talking, I inquired about Sandi's work hours and was informed that she started work about 9. If our presence had crossed, curiosity would have killed the cat and I would have made sure to walk by her office to get an anonymous glimpse of the person with whom I was having this strange phone relationship.

Past experience had taught me to be cautious about women who I'd talked to on the phone and never met. Fantasy often exceeded reality. When reality finally slapped me in the face, I then wished that I hadn't moved from fantasy to reality.

There were exceptions however. Sometimes reality did indeed measure up to fantasy, and when it did, it was really worth crossing the line.

Susan Nichols. The human resources secretary for the company I'd gone to work for in Dallas. When she'd called me 3 or 4 times to give me the specifics on my initial interview in Dallas, I thought she'd had the sexiest voice I'd ever heard. Always a sucker for a Southern Belle, her syrup-sweet drawl could turn me into a stuttering idiot within a matter of moments. Why was it that when a women spoke in a Southern drawl, I decided she was cute or sexy, but when a man spoke in a Southern drawl, I thought he was an uneducated hillbilly from them thar hills? I realized that the logic I used in the initial impressions I formed was lacking.

On my flight from Minneapolis to Dallas for the interview, I'd thought about the marketing job that was available, but I'd also wondered what Susan Nichols would look like. There's no way she would look as good as she sounded, but it would nonetheless be nice to be able to match the face with the friendly voice.

When I finally met Susan Nichols in the lobby of the company I would soon go to work for, she'd immediately proven my suspicions wrong. She was drop-dead gorgeous. One of the prettiest faces I'd ever seen. Wow.

"Welcome to Dallas, Tom. Nice to finally meet you", she smiled as she reached out her hand to greet me.

After I'd accepted the position in Dallas, my eye for talent was soon confirmed when she was selected to be the personal assistant for the chairman of the board. She was also awarded a bit part on the TV show "Dallas" and made a number of appearances, drawl and all. Even if she was out of my league, it was good to see my assessment of her beauty and charm validated.

I never got to know Susan very well after I moved to Dallas. Her new position landed her on executive row and I'd decided that it probably wouldn't be wise to chat her up in front of the chairman of the board's office.

It wasn't long after Susan's promotion before she was involved in a career-threatening scuffle near her desk. It was lunchtime. The office was almost deserted. My racquetball friend Charlie, one of the corporate attorneys and manager of our company's softball team, was walking the offices, making sure he had enough players for our weekly game in Richardson.

It was during his lunchtime walk-around when he stumbled upon two very attractive young women wrestling in the middle of the floor between the president's office and the chairman's office. As Charlie described it, it was a ruckus that could have been a World Wrestling Federation main event. Although flying dropkicks, half-nelsons, and head-butts were not involved, Charlie swore he witnessed a well-executed piledriver.

Charlie immediately recognized the two combatants. One of the women was the previously-mentioned Susan Nichols; the other was the young trophy wife of the chairman of the board. As the fur was flyin', Charlie wasn't sure about what to do. He would have preferred not to have stumbled upon this donny-brook, but the women had already seen him and they both knew him by name.

"Ladies, ladies, ladies. C'mon, let's break it up. This is a place of business", Charlie said as he stepped between them.

It was later revealed that the chairman of the board's wife had accused Susan Nichols of improprieties with her husband…and the wife was bound and determined to do something about it.

Soon after, Susan Nichols was sent walking with what was rumored to be a very nice severance package. She was replaced by a burly middle-aged woman who wore half-socks. This new assistant was also an aspiring model. She was an aspiring model of efficiency. More importantly, she was someone who the chairman of the board's wife would not challenge to a wrestling match.

Too bad about Susan Nichols, I thought. Maybe I'd see her on TV again sometime.

I wondered if there was any chance that Premier Club Sandi could look like Susan Nichols. Sandi and I continued to speak every Wednesday morning for over two months. Finally, I realized that I was embarrassing myself and decided to put an end to the charade. It was time to join the Premier Club. When Sandi asked me, "Are you ready?" for the umpteenth time at the end of one of our phone conversations, I answered with, "Yes, I believe I am, madam. Let's do it."

"Well, I'll be darned. Did you just say what I thought you said, Symalla? Golly gee, it looks like I finally beat you down. Looks like I'm now on the road to a successful sales career. Holly-lou-ya. Looks like I'll be biddin' adieu to that rundown trailer park I've been livin' in. Amazing Grace, how sweet it is."

When the sarcasm had ended, we agreed to meet in her office at noon on the following Tuesday. "I'll be there with pants on", I promised.

"I don't care about the pants. Just make sure you bring your wallet, sucker."

In the days leading up to our meeting, I often wondered, even fantasized, about what it would be like to finally meet Sandi. It was like I was in middle school again. It had been a long time since I'd had the chemistry I'd had with her, even if it was only a Southwestern Bell relationship.

Maybe we were soul mates. Maybe we'd be just as attracted to each other when we finally met. Maybe we'd tell our grandkids this story. The pessimist in me kept me from getting totally carried away, but I was intrigued nonetheless.

On the morning of the much-anticipated meeting, I admitted that I'd become a bit nervous. In an effort to swing the odds in my favor, I wore my most expensive suit, changed my underwear four days before the end of the month, slapped on a healthy dose of Old Spice, and made sure my fly was engaged. I wanted to do whatever was necessary to make a good impression.

In the lobby of the Premier Club, the receptionist told me to take a seat. Sandi was on the phone and the receptionist would escort me to Sandi's office temporarily.

Temporarily came all too soon and the receptionist led me to Sandi's office.

"Tom Symalla. Nice to finally meet you", as we exchanged a hollow handshake.

"Hey, Sandi. It's nice to meet you too."

The in-depth phone conversations we'd had morphed into meaningless, polite small talk when we finally met.

I signed the membership papers and was out of her office in less than 10 minutes, much shorter than any of our soulful conversations.

As I boarded the elevator on the way to my car, I acknowledged that finally joining the Premier Club was a good decision. It was a nice club and my membership would save on all of the guest fees I had been paying. I also acknowledged that fantasy often exceeds reality. Yes, we could have continued to dance, but we both knew the song was over.

Everyone Gets An Earful

Cold Spring, Minnesota. Summer of 1968. After discovering that her eight-year-old daughter Joan had wandered off to the grocery store without permission, my mom was furious.

"You just wait 'til she gets home", Mom warned my sister Barb and I. "She's really going to get an earful."

Sharing a private smile, Barb and I tried to contain our glee. Joan was the baby of our family. Our parents' prized creation. Their final crescendo.

There was a lot of yelling that went on in our house. But the yelling seldom involved baby sister Joan, who apparently had a halo above her head that was visible only to our parents. OK, maybe she didn't deserve to be yelled at as much as Barb and I. Maybe my parents had grown weary of yelling by the time they got to Joan. Or maybe they decided to try a different approach with Joan because the vocal approach they had taken with Barb and I wasn't working. Anyway, whenever Joan got yelled at in the Symalla family household, it was breaking news.

Now, as Mom paced the kitchen floor, awaiting Joan's return, I tried to remember the last time Joan had been yelled at. Must have been when she'd eaten the frog legs which Johnny Vogt had cooked over the garbage can just a few yards from the old cornfield where my friends and I played ball.

Johnny had caught a batch of frogs near Bandy Lauer's garden and he'd decided to treat some of the neighbor kids to an impromptu frog fry and burn the family garbage at the same time. It was multi-tasking as its best. Joan had been a willing participant, snacking on the miniscule morsels that were cooked over the fire in the large metal barrel that was used to burn the Vogt family garbage.

She'd taken an immediate liking to the frog legs. When my mom found out that Joan was eating food cooked over a garbage incinerator, Mom was bewildered. "Don't we feed you enough at home, young lady? You eat frogs cooked over the garbage can at the neighbors, but you won't eat the meatloaf I cook at home? I slave over a hot stove all day every day and you prefer to eat out of the neighbors garbage can? That can't be good for you. You say you want an Easy-Bake Oven for Christmas? Well, maybe we should just go downtown to Wenner's Hardware and get you a garbage can instead? Then you can do all the cooking you want."

As Mom anxiously awaited Joan's return from the town grocery store, I saw an opportunity to test the range of the new Panasonic tape recorder which I'd received for my birthday. As a 15-year-old, my tape recorder was the first of many electronic gadgets to which I'd become attached.

Now that my boyhood aspirations to be a professional baseball player had been squashed by my inability to identify and hit a curveball, I thought that maybe I'd grow up to be a baseball play-by-play announcer. Maybe I'd be another Herb Carneal, Vin Scully, or Ernie Harwell.

I practiced my play-by-play. The Twins against the Cubs in the World Series. My two favorite teams. "Ernie Banks at the plate for the Cubs. Bases loaded. Two outs. Bottom of the ninth. Wrigley Field. Twins leading, 4-1. Jim Kaat, one out away from a complete game. 3-2 count. Kaat will pitch out of the stretch to hold the runners, who will be off with the pitch. Kaat, into his motion, checks the runners, here's the pitch. Banks swings. It's a long drive to left. It's way back. It's way back. It's going. It's going. It's gone! Grand slam for Ernie Banks! Cubs win! Cubs win! Cubs win!"

Even then, I liked to hear myself talk.

I'd even used my new tape recorder to mimic some of my favorite rock and roll songs. Surfin' Bird by the Trashmen was one of my favorites, maybe because the lyrics were easy to remember. "A-well, a everybody's heard about the bird, b-b-b-bird, bird, bird, b-bird is the word..."

In listening back to the songs I recorded, I quickly realized that I was no Mick Jagger, no Peter Townsend, no John Lennon. Either the sound quality on my tape recorder wasn't very good or I was a squeaky-voiced kid with no musical talent.

Now, unbeknownst to Mom, I placed the tape recorder in the cubbyhole near the side door, where Joan would soon return from her trip to Peters Market. The tape recorder was rewound and ready to capture the upcoming hysteria. All I had to do was turn it on just before Joan walked through the door.

Normally, the kids in our family who weren't getting yelled at were sent to their rooms to preserve some modicum of dignity for the kid who was getting yelled at. Barb and I were surprised not to be sent to our rooms. We weren't sure why Mom was allowing us to witness the histrionics. Maybe she viewed it as a teachable moment. Maybe she wanted to prove that she wasn't above reading the riot act to her baby. Maybe she had just forgotten to send us on our merry way. Either way, Barb and I were delighted to have front row tickets to the show. It was going to be more entertaining than Meadowlark Lemon and the Harlem Globetrotters.

Eventually, Mom spotted Joan at the end of our block. Barb and I looked out the window and watched as Joan lollygagged her way toward the impending ambush. Mom was still fuming and Joan was really going to get a piece of Mom's mind. With Joan due to walk through the door at any moment, I reached inconspicuously into the cubbyhole and clicked on the tape recorder. As mad as Mom was, I knew that the volume on the tape recorder was not going to be a problem.

"Where have you been, young lady?", Mom greeted an unsuspecting Joan as she walked through the door. "I've been worried sick."

"I went to the store to get a Snickers bar."

"You didn't ask me if you could go downtown? How many times have I told you kids that you need to tell me when you are going somewhere? And, young lady, you're not old enough to go downtown by yourself. With all the traffic on Highway 23, you could get yourself run over. You should know better..."

The lecture went on and on and on. Mom did all the talking. I was worried that my 30-minute tape was going to run out and then the tape recorder would make a noise. But, finally, the diatribe ended with a "Go to your room, young lady, and think about what you've done. We'll see what your father has to say about this when he gets home."

As Mom followed my little sister to her room, I was almost gleeful as I turned off the recorder and moved it from the cubbyhole to the garage. I promptly verified that Mom's performance had been captured on tape. Those were days before Memorex, I think, but the recording quality on the tape would have done Memorex proud. Crystal clear, just as if the listener was in the middle of the fray.

The neighborhood kids were supposed to play whiffleball that evening. I promised a special treat after the game. Although I offered few hints of what the treat would be, I told everyone that I had something on my tape recorder that they'd just have to hear.

That night, all of the neighbor kids gathered around Krebsbach's picnic table to hear Mom's tirade...one, two, three times. The other kids thought it was great entertainment. Some even went away thinking that maybe their moms weren't so bad after all.

The next day, when Mom was next door, Mrs. Krebsbach smiled and said, "Gee, you really had your dander up yesterday. You must have really been mad at Joan."

Mom was surprised to hear that Mrs. Krebsbach knew about the tongue-lashing she had administered. "Yes, I was really mad at her, but how did you hear about it? You didn't hear me all the way over here, did you?"

"No. No. Tom played the tape for all the neighbor kids last night. All the kids were gathered around the picnic table and I thought I'd see what they were up to."

"You're kidding? You're kidding me? Tom? That Tom. I don't know what I'm going to do with that frutz."

Upon her return from her visit with Mrs. Krebsbach, Mom promptly informed me that I'd have to erase the tape. I objected, but was quickly reminded that the household I lived in was not a democracy. I had hoped to be able to play the tape for my aunts and uncles or for my mom's bridge club...or at least threaten to play it and use it as leverage for future favors, but I was told I'd have to erase the tape if I wanted to continue to live under the same roof as my parents and sisters. The parents and sisters I probably could have done without, but, as a teenaged boy, I'd developed an on-going relationship with the family refrigerator. I erased the tape.

From that day forward, yelling at us kids was different for Mom. Oh, we still misbehaved, and she still yelled at us for doing so, but she was never quite sure if that day's scolding would become the next day's entertainment.

Foiled

Common criminals crammed inside Struzyk's bucket of bolts, we'd trolled through the alleys of upscale Highland Park, looking for open garage doors. If we could just find a long ladder to borrow, we'd be on our way to nearby College of St. Catherine, where we hoped to pull off the heist we'd talked about for days.

"What the hell. Doesn't anybody in Highland leave their garage open? I thought this was supposed to be a low crime area?"

"Would you leave your garage door open if you knew that vicious criminals like us roamed the neighborhood at night?"

"If we don't find a ladder soon, we're going to have to abort this mission. I have to cram for a chem test tomorrow."

"Chem test or not, Hodie, if we find a ladder, we have to bring it back. That's part of the deal."

"Yeah, sure, Tommy. Who are you? Little Goody Two-Shoes?"

"Well, that's the deal, Hoederman. We steal a ladder, we bring it back."

"Hey, if we can't find a ladder, maybe we can build a human ladder. Hell, we have six guys. Think we could reach third floor Stanton by standing on each other's shoulders?"

"Stop, Struzyk. Stop. Bingo. Doesn't look like we'll be doing a cheerleader's pyramid after all, boys. There's the long, tall beauty we've been looking for. I'll be damned if that's not an extension ladder."

Hodie, Mullen, and Coz piled out of the car immediately, unhitching the aluminum ladder that had been hooked to the wall of an open garage.

"Hurry", Struzyk prodded in hushed tones. "Get the ladder and let's get out of here before someone sees us and calls the cops. Not the driver's side, you morons. The passenger side. And don't let the ladder touch my car. I don't want any more scratches on my car, you numbskulls."

Only four blocks from the St. Kate's campus, our motley crew of Tommies headed slowly toward the intended crime scene.

"Geez, I hope we don't see any cops", agonized Struzyk.

"If we do, we'll have some 'splainin' to do, Lucy."

"No shit, Ricky. Six guys in a car in the middle of the night with an extension ladder hanging from the side. You think the cops would think we're up to something?"

But the gods of petty larceny and hijinx were with us and we pulled into the CSC parking lot without interruption.

Stanton Hall, home to a group of unsuspecting Katies, was less than a hundred yards away. We hustled the ladder to the side of the dorm, where we were sure to be out of sight from any Katies returning from late-night dates or study sessions.

It was Swing Era Week on the campuses of St. Thomas and St. Kate's. It had been a week filled with so-called 1930's activities, including swing dance lessons, a pie-eating contest, and a goldfish-eating contest.

Ron Ormberg, a Tommy football player, had won the pie-eating contest, inhaling two chocolate cream pies in less than three minutes.

Our guy Tim Winstone, aka Stoney, had assured us that he and his iron stomach would win the goldfish-eating contest. A human garbage disposal, Stoney would swallow slippery slimy goldfish after slippery slimy goldfish until all of his competition had begged, "no mas, no mas". At least that's what he told us before the contest started.

In front of Murray Hall, we had cheered with pride as Stoney got off to a rousing start, sucking down three small flopping fish before any of his competitors had started their second. We were already envisioning another trophy for Ireland Hall.

Visions premature, after about the 20th fish, some of Stoney's fish decided to swim upstream instead of downstream. When a couple of the fish eventually reappeared, Stoney was disqualified…and a bit green around the gills.

We were disappointed that Stoney had let us down, but when competitor Joe Kustritz blew away the competition by eating 115 goldfish, we knew Stoney never had a fighting chance. But, then again, neither did any of the goldfish.

For days after the contest, we all swore that Stoney had fish breath that may have rivaled Sparky the Seal at the Como Park Zoo.

Just the night before the goldfish-eating contest, an unsanctioned Swing Era Week event had taken place. It all started when a couple of carloads of Katies had been foolishly stopped by St. Thomas security guards before they could streak the area in front of Dowling Hall. The security guards would never hear the end of their Barney Fifedom from the St. Thomas students they were supposed to protect and serve. As far as we were concerned, the security guards should have let the Katies streak to their hearts' content. After all, most of us thought that the presence of nude women could add to the ambience of just about any event.

In response to the failed streak attempt, a group of Tommies had organized an impromptu panty raid on the St. Catherine's campus. As some of my dorm mates prepared to venture a couple miles down Cleveland Avenue to secure their own pair of ladies' panties, I gracefully bowed out, reminding them that I had an article to finish for the next edition of the campus newspaper. This was a reasonable excuse for not participating. I never unveiled my fear of barging into an unfamiliar room in Whitby Hall, only to be confronted by a big, belligerent Katie who wouldn't take kindly to my idea that I should have a pair of her panties, even if I only intended to use them as a pup tent for my summer camping expeditions. She'd give me a wedgie and send me shamefully back to Ireland Hall. As my dorm mates headed to St. Kate's without me, I decided that I'd be better off buying ladies' panties from the back of a magazine, just like I always did.

I was still writing my article for The Aquin when the guys returned, many of them wearing cotton, satin, or laced trophies on their heads. Tom Grabowski, a linebacker on the football team, had been one of the guys who spearheaded the escapade to St. Kate's. A muscular, massive hulk with thick black-rimmed glasses, young Grabowski had intended to use the restroom on second floor Whitby before he began looking for his cloth trophy. Unfortunately for him, he stumbled upon a Katie who was taking a shower. Not quite sure what was going on, the angry Katie wailed a bar of soap at Grabowski. She nailed him smack between the eyes, sending him and his broken glasses tumbling to the floor.

Grabowski, who couldn't see anything without his glasses, was forced to spend his remaining time in the ladies bathroom on hands and knees, trying to find the missing pieces of his broken glasses while a young woman wrapped in a towel screamed and pounded at him.

Returning to Ireland Hall with a glowing welt on his forehead and a pair of thick black-rimmed glasses held together by athletic tape, Grabowski was the butt of all kinds of jokes that night and the next day at breakfast. "Our outside linebacker gets the shit kicked out of him by a Katie. No wonder our football team isn't any good."

But that was then and this was now. Now, as we assembled in the dark of the night beside Stanton Hall, we were part of the Lavinelli family, an Ireland Hall family formed as part of that week's Godfather Contest. The Stantonini family from the College of St. Kate's was the only all-female family formed for the week's festivities. The women of third floor Stanton were our female counterparts and they were frequently our party partners in various extracurricular activities. Kate, Libby, Jenny, Hotzie, Nancy. They were all friends. Friends who were displaying a huge Italian flag from a third floor window of Stanton

Hall. This red, white, and green flag was the prize we coveted. That flag would look spectacular hanging from fourth floor Ireland Hall, we had decided. It would be a constant reminder that the Lavinelli family was not a family to mess with and that we had once again outwitted the group of clueless broads from Stanton Hall.

No Katies in sight, Struzyk gave us the signal to proceed. We hustled the extension ladder to the front of Stanton Hall, directly under the window that displayed the Italian flag that would soon be ours. Hodie had been designated the flag-fetcher. A 6'4" basketball player, he had the wingspan of a condor and could be up and down the ladder faster than any of us, we figured. The rest of us stood below the ladder as Hodie scrambled up toward the third floor window. The damn ladder squeaked more than we had planned, but that was a pitfall of borrowing someone else's ladder. There were no money-back guarantees with stolen merchandise.

We tried to contain our glee as Hoederman began to unhook the flag from the window. Within seconds, the flag would be on its way to St. Thomas. Our friends from Stanton Hall would wake up the next morning, left to wonder what had happened to their precious flag. In future days, one of them would notice it hanging in its glory from fourth floor Ireland Hall and they'd realize immediately that they'd been stung by the Lavinelli family.

Just two more hooks to go and we'd have the designated treasure. We were all standing beneath the ladder when the dorm window opened and buckets of liquid pelted Hoederman and rained down on us. A chorus of giggling Katies announced their presence. Hodie, clung to the window sill, afraid that his adversaries were going to push the ladder backwards and send him crashing to the ground. Finally, without regard for his family heirloom or the Italian flag, Hodie slid down the ladder like it was a firehouse pole. Laughing hysterically, the Stantonini's pulled their flag to safety.

"Nice try, boys", emphasis on the word boys. "Foiled again, boys", emphasis on the word boys. "Have a nice night, boys." The giggles and guffaws from the third story continued, interspersed with ruthless taunting and degradation.

Distraught, defeated, and soaking wet, we eventually slunk back to Struzyk's car. Swear words and bewilderment abounded, as we bemoaned our failure. "Damn broads. They duped us. What the hell happened? Someone must have tipped them off."

Ladder in tow, we now had to worry about returning our borrowed ladder without getting caught. Those Stanton broads. They had outsmarted us once again. We wouldn't have been surprised if they had called the cops to give them a tip about a carload of stooges heading south on Fairview Avenue with a stolen ladder.

Running Away

When my parents visited recently, I was surprised to find that they had forgotten to make the bed they'd slept in. As I made their bed after they had left for home, I smiled as I made a mental note to point out this impropriety the next time I talked to them.

In the home where I grew up, my mother had deemed the failure to make one's bed as a gross misdemeanor. I was indicted for this offense multiple times, but one time stands out in particular:

"Thomas Michael!". My mom's raised voice echoed from my bedroom as she interrupted a morning rerun of *The Andy Griffith Show*. Andy was advising young Opie on the importance of standing up to the school bully, who had been pirating the nickels which Opie had been given for his daily school lunches. Sometimes you just have to stand up for yourself, Andy told Opie, even if the consequences might be painful.

Mom was in no mood to wait for the next commercial. "Thomas Michael. How many times do I have to tell you to make your bed?"

"I don't know", I responded, knowing full well that I couldn't count that high.

I hated making my bed. It wasn't that it was a lot of work or that it took a lot of time. I just never saw the point of it. Why make your bed when you were going to have to unmake it again in another 15 or 16 hours? It just didn't make any sense to me. A waste of time, I thought.

As an eight-year-old, I was going to grow up to be a professional baseball player. One of the biggest perks of being a professional baseball player would be that I would live in a hotel, where maids would be responsible for making my bed. I'd be the favorite guest of all the maids, because I'd tell them they wouldn't have to bother to make my bed. Except when my mom was due to visit, of course.

"Aah, Mom. Why do I have to make my bed? Dave and Johnny Vogt don't have to make their beds. Peter and Stevie Meyer don't have to make their beds." I really didn't know if my baseball buddies had to make their beds or not, but I was hoping to lay a guilt trip on my insistent mother.

It didn't work. "Well, young man. You're not David or Johnny Vogt. And you're not Peter or Stevie Meyer. As long as you're living under this roof, you'll make your bed."

Mom was being extremely unreasonable, expecting me to do my share of the household chores. "But I don't want to make my bed", I responded adamantly.

"Well, if you're not willing to pitch in around here, then maybe you should find some place else to live."

"Well, maybe I'll just do that. I can for sure find a better place to live than here. Maybe I'll run away."

"Fine. If you think you can find a family that will put up with you, I'll even help you pack."

This started a game of blink between my mom and I.

I'd dressed as a hobo the previous Halloween and I remembered the whereabouts of the red kerchief which I had used for a knapsack

My younger sister Barb looked on as I packed some of my favorite baseball cards, my lucky four-leaf clover, and the Huckleberry Hound spoon I had ordered from a cereal box.

My mom contributed to the charade by making me a minced ham sandwich for my upcoming trip. It was drama at its best.

When I'd finished tying my knapsack, I said goodbye to my sister Barb and told her to make sure to feed my dog Blackie. I made sure not to say goodbye to my mom. A man's gotta do what a man's gotta do, I told myself as I stepped out the door.

I immediately appreciated my newfound freedom. I was now in a world where I wouldn't have to wash or wipe dishes, mow the lawn, weed the raspberry patch, or make my bed.

As the mother I'd abandoned watched through the kitchen window, I walked slowly toward Zastrow's bridge without a care in the world. The Sauk River was about three blocks from our house and I knew that my mom wanted nothing to do with the river. Just months before, four-year-old Barb had wandered away from home and headed for the river. We found her before she got there, but my mom's fear of losing a child to the river had been exposed and I was ready to exploit this fear.

As I walked down the block, I realized that I'd have to decide where to go. I was sure that almost anybody would be happy to have me, but then again maybe I wasn't the bargain I thought I was. My grandparents lived only a block away and they were very nice. Grandma would offer me some fresh-baked cookies and Grandpa would tell me some stories. But Mom would expect me to go to my grandparents and they'd eventually have to turn me over to the custody of my mom.

My Aunt Nellie lived in St. Cloud, the city 16 miles away. I could hitchhike to St. Cloud and when I got there, I could probably remember how to get to her house. She was nice too and she had lots of kids…enough kids so that she probably wouldn't notice if one of the kids didn't make his bed.

As I continued toward Zastrow's Bridge along Red River Avenue, I had already decided I was hungry. I'd wait until I crossed the bridge and then I'd rest in the shade under the bridge and eat the sandwich from my knapsack. After that, I'd look for turtles along the river bank. It was a sunny day, the turtles would be sure to be sunning themselves on the rocks and logs along the shore, and I'd find one to take with me, wherever I was going.

Just before I reached the bridge, an old green Plymouth I was very familiar with pulled up beside me. Determined to push forward, I pretended not to hear the words from the woman driving the old green Plymouth.

"Get in the car", she said. "Thomas Michael, get in the car. You're not running away."

"Well if I'm not running away, why did you make me a sandwich?"

I tried not to make eye contact, but eventually I did. When I did, I could see that Mom was concerned that I really might be running away. Game over, she had blinked.

After a couple more minutes of coaxing, my mom's voice finally softened and I thought that she might have even been holding back a smile. I pretended to be reluctant as I climbed into the back seat of our old green Plymouth. As a kid, I sat in the front seat when I liked my mom. I sat in the back seat when I didn't.

Home again, I ate my sandwich, celebrating my victory in a test of wills. Even though Mom wasn't always reasonable, she was very good at making sandwiches. I didn't have to make my bed that day and Mom didn't press the issue. The next day and most days after, I made my bed without being told to do so.

That was the only time I ran away from home…if you can consider three blocks and 10 minutes running away. As I look back on that day, I think I learned more about running away than I learned about making my bed. As an adult, I still don't always make my bed. As for running away from home, I think I realized then that one of the most important things about running away from home is whether someone cares enough to come after you.

Of Woodchucks, Catnaps, and Driver's Ed

It was my last driver's ed session before I'd take my road test. A sign that he was comfortable with my driving, Mr. Bjelland had fallen asleep in the passenger seat as we headed toward the little town of Watkins.

Seduced by the thought of the freedom I'd soon have when I got my driver's license, I put the pedal to the metal as we moved quickly past the dairy farms that decorated the countryside. With a bit of a lead foot, I knew I'd have to tone it down when I took my road test. If I could just get my driver's license, I'd be well on my way toward adulthood. I didn't realize then that adulthood wasn't all it was cracked up to be.

But I didn't want to go too slow either. My friend Wally Westrum had driven too slow when he took his road test. As a matter of fact, he drove so slow that the policeman administering the test had told Wally, "Son, if you don't go a little faster, I'm going to get out of the car and walk beside it. Might as well get some exercise while I'm at it." This statement had flustered the young Westrum. Soon after, he was exceeding the speed limit and his test ended abruptly with another scolding from the officer.

As Mr. Bjelland enjoyed a light nap after what must have been a heavy lunch on a warm summer's day, I thought about when he'd been the supervisor for our elementary school baseball league. Mr. Bjelland was usually the only adult at the games. He was the summer Parks and Rec Director. He hired high school kids to do the umpiring. The games were played on weekday mornings when most adults were working. The players either walked or rode their bikes to the Cold Spring youth baseball park. Cold Spring was a small town and everything was within walking or biking distance for everyone except the farmers.

Mr. Bjelland was a tall, athletic man. He had a gruff exterior, but it masked a soft side.

It was just another ballgame until I came to bat that June morning. Our Braves team was comfortably in first place and we were well on our way to another victory. In the first pitch of this at-bat, I lined a ball into left field. Renowned power hitter that I was, the opposing team's left fielder was playing only about 15 feet behind the shortstop.

With another apparent base hit on this day, I lollygagged my way to first base. I couldn't wait to get home to tell my parents and my sisters that my batting average was again over .350. It wouldn't be long before major league scouts would be stepping all over themselves for a chance to see me play.

Rob Konz was the opposing team's left fielder that day. He had a cannon for an arm. He fielded my line drive on one hop and threw a shot to first base, beating me by a step. I had taken my sweet time in getting to first base and Rob Konz had done the unthinkable. He threw me out from left field. Astonished, I jumped up and down and then buried my face in my hands.

I thought Mr. Bjelland was going to laugh himself to death. He laughed so hard he was crying. "Symalla, I thought I'd seen it all", he roared. "But that's the first time I've ever seen a left fielder throw out a runner going to first base." Big baseball fan that I was, I'd never seen this happen either and I haven't seen it since. I've seen right fielders throw out runners at first base, but never a left fielder. In future at-bats, I tried to ignore the infield taunts encouraging me to get the piano off my back.

Now, as we were halfway to Watkins and I was five years older, I had to laugh myself at what had gone on that day. At first, I had been mad when Mr. Bjelland had such a good laugh at my expense. But I soon realized that it would have been worse if he hadn't acknowledged my gaffe. It was all part of growing up. As a grade school kid who lived and breathed baseball, I knew better than to play "Skip to my Lou" on the way to first base and I never did it again. Lesson learned.

The driver's ed cars were new cars from Kiess Chevrolet and they seemed much faster than my parents' '62 Chevy Impala. Enjoy it while you can, I thought to myself as I raced through the countryside with Mr. Bjelland catching zzzzz's in the passenger seat.

Just as I was about to think again how great it would be to soon have my license, the road in front of me became occupied by a plump furry creature out for a Sunday walk on a Tuesday afternoon. I recognized it immediately as a woodchuck, like those that had lived under the dance hall. With another car approaching in the left lane and a deep ditch looming on the right, swerving was not an option. In a split second, I had to decide if I should hit the brakes and try to spare the life of the chubby chuck. If I did, I knew that Mr. Bjelland's nap would be promptly interrupted by the windshield in front of him. Unlike the Little League play I had just revisited, he'd probably not find my sudden stop so funny.

I clenched my teeth as we drove toward the woodchuck. I hoped he would avoid the underside of the driver's ed car. But he was too fat and not very nimble. The loud thump that followed signaled his demise.

"What the hell was that?", bellowed an awakened Mr. Bjelland. "What did you hit, Symalla?"

"Uh, I think I hit a woodchuck, Mr. Bjelland."

"You think you hit a woodchuck? Well, judging from the sound of it, I don't think there's any damn doubt that you hit something. Why in the hell did you hit a woodchuck? Couldn't you have stopped to let it cross? Couldn't you have moved over into the other lane. Damn, Symalla. What in the world were you thinking?"

"I don't know, Mr. Bjelland. I guess I wasn't thinking."

I waited until Mr. Bjelland calmed down before I told him why I hadn't swerved or why I hadn't hit the brakes. "It was him or you", I pointed out. "And I figured you would have thought you were higher on the food chain." Mr. Bjelland cracked a reluctant smile.

We reached Watkins, turned around and headed back toward the high school in Cold Spring. His nap regrettably behind him, Mr. Bjelland was at full attention the rest of the way home. We passed the scene of the accident and I pointed out the dead woodchuck in the middle of the road. This was a woodchuck that wouldn't chuck wood anymore. Crows in the sky were already circling, waiting for an opening to check out their next meal.

Weeks later, I took my road test in Paynesville. By the time I took it, I was obsessed with thoughts of going too fast or going too slow. I thought about going too fast, nailing woodchucks or anything else that got in my way. I thought about Wally Westrum's experience of going too slow, picturing the policeman walking beside the car. I had nightmares of going too slow. Paynesville kids were waving as they passed my '62 Chevy on their scooters. The Paynesville marching band lapped me as they practiced for the Glenwood Waterama.

As the policeman sat next to me during my road test, my eyes were glued to the speedometer. Traffic signals, turn lanes, and stop signs weren't as important as going too fast or too slow. When I finally rolled through a stop sign, my test ended prematurely.

In a weird sort of way, maybe this was a form of justice for the family of the dead woodchuck.

You Don't Know When, You Don't Know Why, But One Thing Is Sure

My Aunt Rosie had prepared another Thanksgiving feast. I always looked forward to a second helping of turkey and dressing, maybe more mashed potatoes and gravy, and an extra dinner roll.

But this Thanksgiving was different. I joked that my eyes were finally smaller than my stomach. The scheduled events of the day after Thanksgiving had left me unsure as to whether I wanted to be with family or to be left alone.

Just a couple weeks before, I had tried to squeeze a final round of golf from a Minnesota autumn. Like the recent rounds that had preceded it, I had noted the shortness of breath and uncharacteristic belching that had appeared during the first couple holes. I admonished myself for being out of shape, even though I knew I had completed a 30-mile bike ride just a month before.

When these symptoms went away on about the third or fourth hole, I temporarily dismissed my concerns.

Days later, I had to climb four flights of stairs when the elevator in a client's office building was out of order. Again I was short of breath and had to rest after two flights. When I finally reached the fourth floor, I was gasping for air and my left arm was tingling like I had slept on it wrong. I knew then that my body was issuing a warning sign.

That day, immediately after my meeting, I was still thinking about my tingling arm and my lack of breath when I decided to drive to the Barnes & Noble bookstore in Highland Park. *The Complete Guide to Symptoms, Illness, and Surgery* confirmed that I was experiencing angina. Consult your doctor immediately, the book said. I decided to call a doctor as soon as I got back to my office.

The diagnostic nurse at the clinic encouraged me to see a doctor as soon as possible and made a same-day appointment. Dr. Larson agreed with my diagnosis that "there might be something wrong with my ticker." He prescribed a blood-thinner and then referred me to a cardiologist for a stress test.

When I called the St. Paul Heart Clinic, the nurse asked me if I'd ever had a stress test. "You obviously haven't seen me play golf", I cracked. "If that's not a stress test, I don't know what is."

She informed me that a stress test in her frame of reference was a simple treadmill test in which I'd have a number of wires attached to my chest to monitor my heart rate. I would walk on the treadmill, my blood pressure would be measured at regular intervals, and the machine would monitor and record the function of my heart and its reaction to increased exertion. As my heart was subjected to a gradually increasing level of exercise when the treadmill went faster and the incline of the treadmill increased, the clinicians would be able to determine if there was a lack of oxygen or an irregular heartbeat which might not show up during regular activity. "It's a valuable test for diagnosing heart disease", the nurse concluded. "Wear comfortable clothes. We'll see you tomorrow, Thomas."

The following day, as I walked the treadmill, Dr. Brody and I both expressed our love/hate relationship with golf as he and his nurse monitored my heart activity. "This isn't a contest", they reminded me. "If you get tired, you can tell us to stop at any time."

As the speed of the treadmill increased, I worked up a good sweat, but there was no shortness of breath.

"We weren't able to detect any problems with the stress test", Dr. Brody explained after the test. "But that doesn't mean there's not a problem. The symptoms usually don't lie. If you're experiencing shortness of breath and angina, you probably have a problem which is going to manifest itself eventually."

"What are my options? What do you recommend?," I inquired.

"We can leave it alone and watch it, but the problem's not likely to go away and you'll be taking the risk that your next warning sign could be a heart attack. Or we can do an angiogram and this will give us a better idea of what the problem is. Do you know what an angiogram is?"

"Yes, I do." Five years before, I had a heart attack in the middle of a racquetball match and had been rushed to a suburban hospital in an ambulance. I had undergone an emergency angiogram which had cleared some minor blockages. Thankfully, there was very little damage to my heart from the heart attack and I had received a clean bill of health after the procedure. The doctors had prescribed a blood-thinner and an aspirin a day. After six months, they said I didn't need to continue to take the blood-thinner. I was happy about that, but I religiously maintained the aspirin-a-day regimen they had strongly recommended.

I agreed with Dr. Brody that the angiogram was the best option for the problems I was now experiencing. I might as well face this thing head-on, I told myself. No sense in having it hang over my head.

The angiogram was scheduled for the Monday before Thanksgiving. The Heart Clinic nurse who briefed me on the procedure informed me that if they found any blockages, they might insert a stent during the procedure to open and keep open any blocked arteries.

I'd be conscious during the procedure. They'd run a tube up the main artery in my leg and they'd then flush some dye through the tube. I'd feel a brief hot flash as the dye was flushed, but other than that, it would be mostly painless. They'd give me something to relax going into the procedure. I'd even be able to watch the monitor beside the table. It wouldn't be like watching ESPN, but I'd find it interesting nonetheless.

Prior to the procedure, as I lay on the table in the angiogram room, one of the doctor's assistants asked me what kind of music I preferred. "We usually let the patient choose something that will help him relax."

"Well, what do you have?", I inquired. If I hadn't been so damn somber, I'd have probably asked if they had some 1910 Fruitgum Company ("Yummy, yummy, yummy, I got love in my tummy") ...or maybe the Cowsills or the Partridge Family. But I didn't feel like trying to be funny. Not then.

"We have classical, rock 'n roll, jazz, country..."

"I'll go for rock 'n roll, if that's OK with you."

"Sure. We have Rolling Stones, Guns N' Roses, AC/DC, Doors, Metallica, Cars, Aerosmith, Boston, Kansas, Journey. Any of those strike your fancy?"

"Yeah. How 'bout some Doors?" It was ironic, I thought, that Jim Morrison had died at an early age. Hopefully, he and I would not have that in common. When the medical technician inserted the tape into the high-tech boom box, I thought it was more ironic that Jim Morrison was encouraging me to "break on through to the other side." It was a bit creepy, I thought, and that particular song wasn't doing much to relax me.

As the procedure progressed, they flushed the dye into my arteries. It hurt more than the last time, but I closed my eyes, grimaced, and the discomfort was quickly gone.

The physician who had performed the angiogram consulted in the background with Dr. Brody, then approached me on the table.

"Thomas, you have a blockage in one of your arteries." He pointed with his finger to an area on the monitor. "It's a fairly long blockage. Looks like it's over two inches long. That explains some of the problems you've been having. We'd normally consider doing an angioplasty or inserting a stent to open the artery, but this blockage is too long."

"So what do we do now? What do you recommend?", I asked.

141

"Well, Thomas. It looks like we're going to have to do a bypass."

"You agree?", I asked Dr. Brody.

He nodded. "I don't think we have any other options. The good news is that it will be a single bypass. You're young and in otherwise good health. There will be some risks, but you should come through it just fine."

"When do you want to do it?"

"Well, we'll have a consult with the surgeon, but we'll want to do it soon. Probably right after Thanksgiving."

"Should we be waiting that long?"

"I don't see any problems in waiting a couple of days. I'll keep you on blood-thinners and I'll give you my pager number in case there's a problem, but I don't think you're in any imminent danger, as long as you don't do anything too stressful in the next couple of days."

"Doc, can you guarantee me that I'll be able to hit a golf ball 300 yards after surgery?", I asked, trying to lighten my own apprehension.

"Well, that will cost extra and I'm not sure your insurance will cover it. But if we do the surgery, and the bypass is successful, you'll be good as new and able to do all the golfing you want."

Angiogram over, I was eventually transported to a hospital room where I was surrounded by an inquiring family and told to keep my leg very still for the next six hours. This was the leg they'd run the tube through.

As I lay there, the nurse brought in a video and asked me to watch it. It explained the bypass procedure that awaited me later in the week. The fact that my heart would stop beating during the surgery was all I needed to know about the seriousness of the operation. The mere mention of a urinary catheter made the thought of a prostate exam or a colonoscopy seem like a day at Valleyfair. Add a chest tube, a throat tube, and the circular saw they'd use to cut through my sternum, and it was a buffet full of my medical nightmares.

I continued to crack jokes throughout the video. I told myself I was doing this to keep my family in good spirits, but I knew that this irreverence was my distorted way of dealing with the seriousness of the matter.

Dismissed from the hospital, the nurse encouraged me to enjoy my Thanksgiving.

"Sure", I said. Sure that I probably wouldn't be able to enjoy my Thanksgiving.

The day after the angiogram, I was at work bright and early. Business as usual, I told myself. I informed my employees of the pending surgery and thanked them in advance for covering for me.

During the days before the bypass, I was focused on clearing up any loose ends, but I was also distracted. At least a couple times a day, I asked myself why I was working. Was it that important for my construction company customer to get their 12 t-shirts in time. If I died in surgery, they'd certainly understand my decision to "go fishing" instead of delivering their order on time. Or was it that important to work on the Video Update sales presentation. Maybe I wouldn't be around to implement the program anyway.

But working on these now seemingly trivial matters helped the time pass quickly, and these would then be things I wouldn't have to worry about if I lived, I decided.

I'd even worked Thanksgiving morning. There were so many loose ends to tie. Dishes that weren't washed, the messy desk in my office, the refrigerator magnet order for the Scholtzsky's Deli in Decatur, Illinois. I even made my bed, not because I usually do, but because, if anything happened to me, I wanted to be remembered as someone who made his bed.

I had been instructed to eat regularly at Thanksgiving. "You mean I should eat like a pig?", I asked. The physician's assistant smiled and then informed me that I should also drink the bottle of Citron she was giving me. I should drink it about 8 p.m. on the night before surgery and it would clean my system of any of the food that I was storing. Unfortunately, winter was coming and I had consumed a lot of food in hopes of hibernation. From what I'd heard about the Citron, I wondered if I should eat the Thursday Thanksgiving dinner or if I'd be better off dumping the plate directly into the commode. I understood that the Citron would escort the food there quickly anyway.

After a modest serving of Thanksgiving dinner, I tried to watch the Vikings-Cowboys game. Normally, I would have been looking forward to this game. The Vikings were in the middle of a great season and most Vikes fans thought they were Super Bowl bound. But now, the game seemed trivial. I left for home at halftime to drink my Citron and to take the first of two required showers with disinfectant soap.

My surgery was scheduled for 7 a.m. I was told to be at the hospital by 5 a.m. That Thanksgiving night, I was glad to be by myself in the hopes that I could come to grips with my emotions and maybe place my 45-year-old life in some sort of perspective.

The TV, however, provided a welcome distraction between bathroom visits. The Vikings blew out the Cowboys. Randy Moss had a helluva game, and John Madden shared his six-legged turkey with some of the Vikings players in the post-game interviews.

"Must See TV" featured an "ER" rerun which I had already seen, but when Dr. Carter cracked open the chest of an emergency patient, the show took on a whole new meaning for me. When Dr. Ross pulled a tube out of a throat, I knew I'd soon be experiencing that. When Dr. Greene lost a patient, I knew that patient could be me tomorrow if things didn't go well.

There's a song that goes

> *Life's a bitch and then you die.*
> *You don't know when and you don't know why.*
> *Fate comes in and throws the switch.*
> *Life's a bitch and then you die.*

From the time I'd found out that I'd be having a bypass, I had tried to remain positive. I had heard the stories that patients with positive attitudes were more likely to survive major surgery than patients who had negative attitudes or who were depressed. I believed those stories, but I still spent too much time fending off ominous, morbid thoughts that were haunting me. Would this be the end of the road? Or was there more road to travel?

It seemed like an eternity before 4:30 a.m., when my dad and my sister Joan picked me up to go to the United Hospital in downtown St. Paul. The hospital was very quiet at that early hour. I checked in and we waited until 5:30, when I was showed to the room where I would be prepped for surgery.

I thought about whether I'd rather be a surgeon's first patient of the day or his last. I decided first was best, especially after what I hoped had been for him a relaxing Thanksgiving holiday. Of course, if my surgeon had too much holiday wine, or if his family had a stressful holiday as some families do, maybe being his first patient of the day wasn't best after all.

The anesthesiologist's assistant came in to introduce herself and tell me what would happen. The anesthesiologist would be in soon to ask me some questions.

A guy came in to shave me. I made nervous conversation until he had finished.

In the bed where the hospital personnel prepared me for surgery, I was in remarkably good spirits. My parents and my sisters were kind enough to smile at my witticisms, but the smiles were nervous smiles just the same.

When the anesthesiologist and his assistant came in, the irreverent front which had masked my fears in previous days disappeared. The one-liners and the quips which had rolled off my tongue all week were no longer available. Forced to face mortality, I wondered what plans it had for me. I admitted to myself that I was scared. Sullen and scared. Very sullen and very scared. This was it.

I had always had a philosophy that I wouldn't worry about things I couldn't control. This philosophy had worked well for me so far, but it wasn't working now as I entrusted my life to a heart surgeon who I had met only five minutes ago. I exchanged *I Love You's* with my family before the anesthetic was administered. I was apparently then wheeled off to surgery.

As I'm writing this story, it shouldn't be a surprise to the reader that I survived this brush with mortality. The surgery was successful.

Soon after the surgery, nurse Robert was quick to make me sit up in bed. I was groggy, I was weak, and my incision hurt like hell.

My post-operative pain eventually subsided. On the Monday following Thanksgiving, I was released on my own recognizance into the custody of my family. The surgical nurse assured me that the new bypass would be good for at least 20 years unless I continued to ingest bacon for breakfast, lunch, and dinner.

As I write about these goings-on, years have passed and I'm feeling fine. I realize now that this heart bypass operation forced me to acknowledge my mortality, maybe for the first time.

Now, as I stand in front of my bathroom mirror after my daily shower, I can't help but notice that the large *S* that once adorned my chest has been replaced. Replaced by an eight-inch scar that is all too willing to remind me. Remind me that I am no longer the invincible, indestructible, immortal young man I once thought I was. I may not know when and I may not know why, but I'll die someday.

The Woolly Mammoth

As part of Mr. Seguin's seventh and eighth grade football team, my aspirations of playing high school football were grinding to a halt. I was short, I was skinny, and I didn't like contact. Also, I was slow, although my speed increased remarkably when someone was chasing me.

It was a late September afternoon at the Cold Spring Municipal Baseball Park, which turned into a football field when the baseball season ended. Our St. Boniface team was hosting Watkins, a team from a neighboring town.

I was on the third string team, only because we didn't have a fourth or fifth string. Our third string unit called ourselves the Scrubeenies, a name derived from scrubs, subs, and weenies. The Scrubeenies played only when games were out of reach. Our first team was very good, so our mop-up squad always saw plenty of action.

This was a time when they didn't separate elementary football players by size. As I watched the first string run over our opponent, I was reminded that these games were much more serious than the sandlot games of tackle football we played behind Guggenbergers' house. Although we didn't wear helmets or pads in those evening pickup games which sometimes ended when someone got hurt and went home crying or limping, no one was ever hurt seriously enough to not want to play the next night.

With this organized football, however, things were different. Early in the game against Watkins, our 210-pound fullback ran right through one of the smaller Watkins players who had tried to tackle him. As we waited for the town ambulance, we found out that the Watkins player had broken his collarbone.

On a day when our team overmatched our opponents in size, speed, and score, the first string played only until halftime. Jim Decker, John Backes, and Tom Kraemer racked up points like a pinball machine before the second team took over in the third quarter.

The game was safely in hand when Mr. Seguin called on us Scrubeenies at the start of the fourth quarter. We sprinted on the the field, eager to claim our part in yet another St. Boni victory.

I was a tight end, which, believe me, made no reference to my physical attributes, but rather meant that my main responsibility was to block opposing players. Occasionally, and this was the fun part, the tight end got to go down the field for a pass.

Before we got in the game against Watkins, I'd lobbied for our quarterback John Dorgan to call a pass play intended for me. I assured him I'd catch his pass and take it all the way for a long touchdown. We'd be the toast of Scrubeenies everywhere.

My pleas fell upon deaf ears and John Dorgan called a running play, relegating me to the role of a blocker. "Break", we yelled and clapped in unison as we broke from the huddle and sprinted up to the line of scrimmage.

"Holy shit", I exclaimed for all to hear as I took my place at the line of scrimmage. Lined up directly in front of me was the biggest kid I had ever seen. Well over 250 pounds, he might have been twice my size. With hairy legs that could have passed as pelts in most trading posts, the mountainous creature in front of me was a spectacular and scary sight. His huge ham hocks would have made a meat market proud, his breasts would have made a Hollywood starlet proud, and his baby face could have been featured on a Gerber jar.

The Woolly Mammoth in front of me snorted his acknowledgment of my feeble presence as we eyed each other. His faceguard looked like a set of tusks. He was panting and breathing heavily from his recent run on to the field. This was a man-child if I ever saw one, I told myself. This was a man-child who had obviously never missed a meal and my biggest fear was that I was his next.

As I bent into my three-point blocking stance, I was proud of the fact that I hadn't yet wet myself. "The bigger they are, the harder they fall", I tried to reassure myself. When that didn't dispel my fears, I started to recite the rosary.

By the time the ball was snapped, I was fearless. Launching myself like a rocket, I tried to block one of the Woolly Mammoth's hairy legs. The Woolly Mammoth swatted me away like I was a pesky gnat. But he was too slow to catch our ball carrier.

This went on play after play as our Scrubeenie squadron marched down the field. I thought about biting the Woolly Mammoth in the knee to put him out of commission, but I couldn't jump that high. I was sure that Mr. Seguin was having quite a chuckle as he watched me try to budge the large mass of blubber that lined up in front of me.

Thankfully, the Woolly Mammoth wasn't mean. Thankfully, he wasn't strong or fast. Thankfully, he never fell on me. The ambulance still wasn't back from taking the kid with the broken collarbone to the St. Cloud Hospital.

Have Thumb, Will Travel

Spontaneous on a sunny spring Saturday, we had organized a sightseeing excursion of St. Paul's historic Summit Avenue. College freshmen from Cold Spring, Rochester, Waseca, and Palatine, Illinois, we were still wide-eyed at the sight of the massive mansions along the Avenue.

Almost every time we'd traversed the Avenue, someone had pointed to another monstrosity. "Wow. Look at that one. I want to live in a mansion like that when I grow up. And look at the size of the guest house. Hell, I'd even settle for the guest house. It's larger than most regular houses. Can you imagine what it costs to heat a place that size?"

No fault of his, I'd never read any of the writings of F. Scott Fitzgerald, although his "Great Gatsby" was next on the agenda for my English lit class. I had read that Fitzgerald had lived on a common part of the Avenue when he was a young man and I wondered if the Avenue had sparked the same astonishment for him that it had for us.

Tuck, Willie, Greg, and I were Ireland Hall dormmates at the College of St. Thomas. None of us had wheels, so we'd agreed to travel by thumb. For CST students without cars, the thumb was an invaluable and inexpensive mode of transport around the city of St. Paul. To those of us who thumb-bummed rides repeatedly, hitchhiking was an art, with tactics and techniques.

Look normal. Look interesting. Look urgent. Look cold. Look harmless. Get out into the street where drivers can't help but notice you. Get out there where drivers will damn near have to stop to avoid running over you. And when you're out there in the street, beware of the guy in the passenger's seat who might open his door and knock you on your ass as the car speeds by. Keep your idle hand out of your pocket, so possible rides won't think you're toting a gun or a knife, or playing pocket pool.

"Hey, we better split up", Tuck was the first to propose a strategy. "Nobody's going to pick up all four of us. We'll do better in twos."

Willie's suggestion that one of us should hitchhike while the other three of us hid behind trees was quickly disregarded.

"Tell you what", Tuck noted, "Tommy and I will run up ahead a block or so and you guys can stay here."

"Yeah, we'll give you two motley mothers first chance to get a ride", I had accentuated our bigheartedness to Willie and Greg. "If someone sees a couple of good-lookin' All-American guys like Tuck and I, you two losers won't stand a chance, unless someone is headed past the detox center."

"Meet you at the cathedral", Tuck had set the destination.

"Yeah, we'll be catching some zzzzz's on the steps by the time you two mopes finally get there", I had reiterated the challenge, laid the gauntlet. "If you guys are too ugly to catch a ride, you might have to take a bus. Make sure you have a couple of quarters for bus fare. Either that or maybe you can find a grocery store that will give you a couple of bags to put over your heads."

"We'll see, boys. We'll see."

As Tuck and I created distance on foot between Willie and Greg, we agreed that our chances of arriving at what had become a finish line weren't very good. All eastbound Summit drivers would have to pass Willie and Greg first. It was unlikely that a driver would neglect Willie and Greg and give us a ride instead.

"The only way we can beat those guys", Tuck, breaking into a jog, "is if we can get far enough away from them and get a ride from a car that's turned on to Summit between them and us. Or else, maybe their ride won't take them all the way to the end of the Avenue and they'll have to thumb a second ride. Let's go, Symalla."

A godsend rewarding eternal optimism, a white Impala pulled over. "Hi, where you fellas headed?", inquired the father of a young son.

"We're going to the cathedral. How's that sound?"

"Fine. Hop in, guys. We're going past the cathedral. We're headed to the hardware store to pick up some lawn fertilizer. Mommy has us working on her honey-do list today, doesn't she Robbie?" The little boy nodded, more fascinated by the two strangers in the back seat.

"Well, don't let her work you too hard", said Tuck. "Hey, did you pass a couple of other hitchhikers two or three blocks up the road?"

"No. We just turned on to Summit at Fairview. Didn't see any other hitchhikers, did we Robbie?"

Exchanging thumbs up signals and simultaneous smiles, Tuck and I knew we'd left Willie and Greg in their tracks. We'd be waiting for them near the end of the Avenue.

After "Thanks for the lift", "Have a nice day", and "Goodbye, Robbie", Tuck and I quickly made ourselves comfortable on the steps of the Cathedral of St. Paul. I'd brought a section of the newspaper with me and I was prepared to drape it over my head in the interests of emulating a nap when our fellow travelers approached.

Ten minutes later, Willie and Greg emerged from a Ford Fairlane.

"Damn, it's about time you guys got here", I bellowed. "You get lost or what? We've been here almost an hour. Another 15 minutes and I'd have grown a beard. And then I'd have looked more like your mom, Willie."

"Yeah, what took you guys so long?", Tuck chimed in.

Braggadocio eventually ran its course, and for sightseeing purposes, we became one again.

Because I'd read a recent article about St. Paul's historic Summit Avenue, and because a little knowledge was dangerous, I immediately anointed myself tour guide and resident historian. Like someone who had actually visited the area before, I was quick to impart vast granules of knowledge as we sauntered past the grandiose structures that had earmarked the society which had flourished in St. Paul in the late 19th and early 20th centuries.

We started inside the cathedral, where I launched into my spiel. "The building of this cathedral was orchestrated by

Archbishop John Ireland. Yep, he's the same cat who our dorm is named after. The cathedral can seat over 3000 minnow munchers. You'll note the copper dome above us. It's one of the things that reminds people of Michelangelo's St. Peter's Cathedral in Rome. And that there is none other than St. Cloud Granite, mined just a few miles from my hometown of Cold Spring, Minnesota."

Leaving the cathedral, we worked our way west to a huge mansion. "This is the famous Hill House. James J. Hill was founder of the Great Northern Railroad. Came here from Toronto. The Hill House was built in the 1890's for more than $1 million smackers. Place is supposed to have 22 fireplaces. See that mansion over there…that was built by a cat who was a buddy-buck associate of Hill. He must have been a cake-eater himself, because he owned a million-dollar racetrack somewhere near the state fairgrounds."

We continued our walk. "This house here was the Weyerhauser pad. That little shanty over there is the Burbank-Livingston-Griggs House. Burbank, like Hill, was another Canuck. He founded a stagecoach line and streetcar company. Stagecoach, that must have been how you two guys finally got here.

"One of the rooms in that house is straight out of a Jean Harlow movie. Another is done like King Louie's sitting room. The house has a bathtub carved out of a single block of granite. Willie, you probably wouldn't recognize a bathtub if you were in one, granite or porcelain. And one of the bedrooms had nothing but mirrors on the walls and ceilings. How'd you like to get laid in there?"

"Where's Fitzgerald's house?"

"Fitzgerald didn't have a house in this neck of the woods. He didn't have a house, period. On the way here, we passed the building where he rented a room in the 1920's. Fitzgerald lived on the unfashionable end of Summit. I think I read something that said he lived in St. Paul for seven years. Young Fitz used to walk past the Hill House and these other mansions all the time. He was apparently fascinated by the filthy rich. That fascination inspired the completion of his first real book. Yep, young Fitz lived only blocks from here, but millions of dollars away."

Eventually cultured out, we decided to hitchhike back to campus. Saturday night was steak night in the Murray Hall cafeteria.

Teams the same, Tuck and I had conceded another headstart to Willie and Greg. "See you guys back at the dorm", I had exuded complacency. "We'll probably be into our second or third beers by the time you unsightly chumps are able to get a ride."

Walking blocks ahead, Tuck and I had reveled in how we'd rub their noses in it if by chance we won again. We had given them another advantage, and if we won again this time, we'd never let them hear the end of it. If we returned to campus last, it was to be expected, as we had done the gentlemanly thing and allowed them the advantage. We realized that we had nothing to lose.

Lost in our glee, Willie put a damper on our merriment when he waved hello-goodbye with his middle finger from the backseat of a car that passed us by. "That asshole", Tuck had acknowledged our deficit.

Mumbling about our misfortunes, we had almost been oblivious to the car that had pulled over to offer us a ride.

"You guys need a ride?", the high school girl from the passenger side yelled out the window.

"Yeah, great. Thanks.", climbing into the back of what must have been the family car.

"Where are you guys going?", asked the other girl, the better looking of the two.

"We're going back to the dorms at St. Thomas or as close as we can get."

"Oh, we're only going up to Snelling, but that will get you pretty close."

Snelling Avenue. About a mile short of St. Thomas. "Oh, that's fine, ladies. We appreciate the ride", realizing that Willie and Greg were probably going to even the score.

Our chauffeurs were both OLP students, they said. Our Lady of Peace, the Catholic girls school on Summit. Or Our Ladies of Piece, as some of the guys on campus had labeled them. They asked us if college was fun. We told them it was, except for all the studying. We asked them if they planned to go to college when they got out of high school. They were nice and we enjoyed some laughs on our Saturday jaunt down Summit.

"Hey, Tommy. You see what I see?", Tuck temporarily turned off the charm to point out Willie and Greg, thumbs out at curbside, obviously in search of a second ride back to campus.

Stopped at the light, rolling down the window, Tuck was quick to harass our dejected dormmates. "Boy, you guys are ugly. What happened? A Mack truck run over you? Hey, you in the letter jacket. What's up with that face? You must have been goalie on your high school dart team. Must have stopped a lot of shots without a goalie's mask."

Easily amused, Tuck and I laughed hysterically.

"You know those guys?", asked our driver. "Should we give them a ride? The taller one is kind of cute."

Afraid that our chauffeurs would tell Tuck and I to get out of the car so there would be room for Willie and Greg, I quickly pointed out that the light was green.

"No, I wouldn't even think of giving those two losers a ride", said Tuck. "Believe me, you want nothing to do with those guys." Tuck rolled up his window and we moved on, still a foursome.

As we drove toward Snelling, Tuck and I let the girls in on our contest. They then understood why we had left our acquaintances rideless, regardless of how cute they were.

Anxious to become part of the game, our new accomplices agreed to go the extra mile and drove us all the way back to Ireland Hall.

Tuck attributed our good fortune to our charm and good looks.

I thought it was just a couple of high school girls who jumped at the chance to tour a men's dormitory.

Either way, it didn't matter. We'd beaten Willie and Greg again. Have thumb. Well-traveled.

Peas, Peas, Peas, Peas

At past family gatherings, my mom has been quick to tell anyone who will listen about my love of peas when I was a baby. I loved them so much that I spit my first spoonful of baby food peas all over the new curtains of the apartment in which we were living.

I later maintained that I was releasing my inner artist, trying to create a mural that would be enjoyed by many. One of the neighbor ladies thought she saw the face of Mary Magdalen in my mural and she was soon conducting religious pilgrimages through our apartment, but I think she got a little carried away. Although I was too young to remember this episode in fine dining, my mom seems to remember it very well.

My look-into-the-future imitation of Linda Blair in "The Exorcist" ended my days of being force-fed Gerber peas and carrots. If only I'd been able to talk, I could have communicated my preference for prime rib with horseradish sauce.

Years later, when I was about 11 years old and my sister Barb was about 7, I suddenly reacquired my taste for peas. Not because I liked them, but because Barb hated them so much.

When my mom would ask me what kind of vegetable we should have for supper, I'd sheepishly reply, "Peas would be good". I knew well that peas would provide hours of viewing pleasure at that night's dinner table.

Barb hated peas and my mom would never let Barb leave the table until she had finished the peas. Barb gagged, whined, cried, and pouted in an effort not to have to eat her peas. She played with the peas, she counted the peas, she complained that she received more peas than me or my sister Joan.

Barb tried everything to get rid of her helping of peas. She hid them under her plate. She placed them on other peoples' plates when she thought they weren't looking. She "unintentionally" dropped them on the floor. She went to the bathroom four times in one meal. When my mom caught on, she wouldn't let Barb flush. Barb even offered to mail the peas to China in an effort to feed the starving children we were always hearing about at the family dinner table.

It was great fun for an 11-year-old boy. And it was a nice distraction from all the things I'd done wrong during the day. I had to pretend not to enjoy Barb's histrionics and facial contortions too much, or mom would discover my real reason for wanting peas for dinner.

In the summer, I would almost always hurry to finish my dinner so I could play sandlot baseball with the boys in my neighborhood. There were times when I played a couple hours of baseball and returned home to find Barb still at the kitchen table with peas that were now growing mold. And mom would still be hovering nearby, in a battle of wills between mother and daughter that no longer had anything to do with peas.

Whenever I got the chance and whenever Mom was out of sight, I'd break into my rendition of my new favorite song: "Peas, peas, peas, peas. Eatin' goober peas. Goodness how delicious. Eatin' goober peas."

Upon hearing my teasing, Barb would turn the color of a beet, another vegetable she didn't like. She would have loved to yell at me, or better yet, she would have loved to squeal to my parents, but her cheeks were either too full of peas or she was too busy retching to rat on me.

Barb was finally excused from the table in time to get a masters degree. At the time of this writing, she works in a pain management program for a local children's hospital. I didn't realize it then, but I now know that Barb's episodes at the kitchen table were great training for her career in pain management.

I've been an appreciative dinner guest at her house many times in recent years. During those dinners, she's served vegetables of all kinds, colors, and shapes. But she appears to be living a life void of peas.

When the reality TV show Fear Factor was on, I wondered how Barb would do as a contestant on the show. The idea of eating cow brains, sheep eyes, pig intestines, and various worm varieties wouldn't have been as intimidating as the thought of having to eat baby peas.

As an adult, I've learned to like a lot of vegetables that I didn't enjoy as a kid. Spinach, asparagus, broccoli, cauliflower. Even cooked carrots.

I'm still not sure how much I like peas, but every time I eat them I smile when I'm reminded of the shows they provided when I was growing up. For an 11-year-old kid, having peas for dinner was as good as going to the circus.

Sure, But Make It Quick

I should have known better. What seemed to be a quick trip to Barnes & Noble to buy a gift card for one of my employees turned into a mini shopping spree for myself.

I hate shopping. A successful shopping trip for me means that I know what I want to buy before I enter the store, I find the item immediately without the help of a sales clerk, and I'm in and out of the store in a span of five minutes.

Maybe it's because I don't like crowds, but I've never liked the concept of shopping. And the thought of shopping without buying something is even more disturbing. If you ask me, it's a downright waste of time.

As a kid, I was tortured every August with a shopping trip for school clothes. If I could have had my way, I would have worn the same clothes that I had worn to school the previous year, but I was a kid, and most of last year's clothes no longer fit. So despite some of my best whining, my mom would haul me to St. Cloud for our annual shopping extravaganza. By the time we were done shopping, it seemed to me like I had tried on every pair of pants, every shirt, and every set of shoes in Crossroads Mall. I wanted to walk directly to the rack or shelf and buy the first thing I liked. My mom wanted to visit multiple stores and have me try on multiple "outfits".

165

These shopping trips were never fun for Mom and I. We always ended up liking each other less than when we had begun. Only the promise of a Sandy's hamburger and fries at the end of the escapade got me through the day. My mom liked to shop; I was a lousy shopping partner. To my mom's credit, and to my benefit, she eventually realized that my sisters were much better shoppers and she drafted them for her shopping trips.

As an adult, I still hate to shop, but I'm quick to acknowledge my weaknesses--Barnes & Noble, Best Buy, or any golf store.

The visit to Barnes & Noble which I've previously referred to is a classic example. I intended to buy a $50 gift card for an employee. I'd be on my way within a matter of minutes, I assured myself as I entered the giant bookstore in Highland Park.

Seduced by the smell of Starbucks coffee and fresh paperbacks, I couldn't help but browse a while. I haven't been a coffee drinker for years, but I still love the smell of coffee. But then again, I also love the smell of stale beer, bratwurst, and cigarettes at an outdoor ballpark. I'm not quite sure what that says about me.

By the time I'd finished my browsing, I needed help carrying the books I had purchased at Barnes & Noble. Self-centered person that I am, I spent $50 on my employee and $100 on myself.

I've done the same thing at Golf Galaxy, where I've gone in to buy a $12 golf glove and left the store with a $200 golf club guaranteed to resurrect my wretched golf game. If only I would heed the advice of my UPS driver and invest in lessons instead of miracle technology.

I'm also reminded of the time many years ago when I went into a Dallas electronics store to buy a Sony Walkman. I expected to spend about $60 for a Walkman. If only I had a Walkman, I told myself, maybe I would start jogging again and I could rid myself of the new belly which I'd been carrying around.

The marketing gurus at the electronics store knew what they were doing when they made their customers walk through the TV section to get to the Walkmans. In an effort to get to the Walkmans, I was immediately mesmerized by the bigness of the big screen televisions. A salesman noticed me salivating and quickly escorted me into the private viewing room, fully equipped with Surround Sound and all of the newest, most expensive television models.

As he ushered me to the leather recliner in front of the big screen TV, I was quick to tell him that I already had a perfectly good TV, he was wasting his precious time, and he wouldn't be selling me a TV today. I just want a Walkman for the new jogging regimen I intend to embark upon.

"Sure, I can show you the Walkmans, but do you have time to see this TV first. It's the largest tube TV model ever made and you won't believe the picture quality."

"Well, if you can make it fast. I have other errands to run after I'm done here, but I suppose it couldn't hurt to see what's new."

The salesman shut the door to the viewing room. "Are you ready?", he asked excitedly.

"Ready for what?", I asked back.

"Ready for a viewing experience like you've never had before", he said, as he turned the video tape to a preset part in the movie *Top Gun,* where all the fighter jets were getting ready to take off from a huge ship in the Indian Ocean.

"Sure, but make it quick", I yelled as the sound immediately engulfed us. The viewing room shook. The noise of the jets was loud and distinct. Tom Cruise and I were standing next to each other and he was shorter than me. The picture quality was the best I had ever seen and the sound was spectacular.

"Damn", I yelled over the jet noises to the smiling salesman. "I feel like I'm there."

I was slobbering all over myself at the thought of adding this large toy to my entertainment collection. I could place it beside the TV I already had and watch two games at the same time. How great would that be? The electronic monstrosity would complement perfectly my plaid couch with the cup holders in the armrests.

Without friends or family there to do an intervention, I couldn't wait to get my wallet out. The salesperson told me he'd waive the delivery charge and make sure my new TV would be delivered the following day. The Surround Sound Team would call me within a matter of days to make an appointment for a sound system evaluation. The TV delivery people would hook up everything for me.

That's great, I thought, admitting to myself that I wasn't very good at setting up electronic devices. I was really good at buying them, but I wasn't good at setting them up. I still hadn't figured out how to set the timer on my VCR. The time display window had stayed at 12 noon for almost three years now. I was OK with that, mostly because it was always lunchtime according to my VCR.

As I exited the television store, I was giddy with the purchase of my humongous state-of-the-art television.

On the drive to my condo, I realized that I'd never even looked at the Sony Walkmans. So much for my new exercise program, I thought to myself. Looks like I'll be spending a lot more time on my couch. I'd spent $3200 on a big screen TV instead of the $60 I'd expected to pay for the Walkman.

Like I said, I hate shopping.

The Bogeyman Cometh

When I was a young boy I had a recurring fear that someone was hiding under my bed. I wasn't sure what he'd look like if I ever met him, but my imaginings made him out to be big and hairy, half man, half animal, all monster. He'd wait until I was asleep and then he'd reach up with his hand and get me.

I always stored as much stuff as possible under my bed in an effort to leave no extra space for my imaginary intruder. Every night before I got into bed, I'd get down on my knees and took a quick look under my bed, just to make sure I was alone.

I found out later that some of the other kids had boogeymen in their closets, and these kids always checked their closets for unwanted occupants before they went to bed. My closet was too messy to provide residence for a boogeyman. My boogeyman was under my bed.

I was a freshman in college. It was a Friday night in September, and it had been a great night for a kegger along the Minneapolis side of the nearby Mississippi River. The party site had been dubbed Bareass Beach, because it was tradition for students, male and female, to moon the barges as they trudged along the mighty river in the dark of night. Sometimes the barge captains would acknowledge our efforts by sounding a foghorn.

After a night of partying, I returned to Ireland Hall with my buddies. Although I hadn't had much to drink, I acknowledged to myself that I was glad Monk and I had finally taken the bunk beds apart. Having two beds on the floor reduced the available space in the crackerbox dorm room even more, but after a few barley pops, it was sometimes a challenge to get into the top bunk.

As I lay me down to sleep, my mind recapped the events of the evening with a myriad of incomplete thoughts: Getting the empty keg up the river bank was a lot easier than getting the full keg down the river bank. Almost got away from us a couple of times. I can't believe Ziggy swam across the river. He could have drowned. Intramural football game Monday against the Brady Bunch. If we win, we make the playoffs. Psych test on Tuesday. I'll have to pull an all-nighter Monday night. The Iowa chicks are great. Jane, Jan, and Mo.

Finally, I drifted to sleep. Never able to sleep on my back or stomach, I always slept on my side, one arm under my pillow.

It was the middle of the night when I opened my eyes to find a hand next to my face. Harkening back to my childhood fears of having a Boogeyman under my bed, I went to touch the hand by my face with my other hand…just to make sure the hand by my face was my own. When I touched the hand by my face, I didn't feel anything in the other hand.

Certain that my childhood phobia had finally materialized, I jumped out of bed, screaming like a banshee. Sprinting to the closet, I grabbed my baseball bat. Still screaming, I began pummeling my mattress with the bat. My baseball coach had often told me I couldn't hit a curveball. He didn't know I could whack the stuffing out of a mattress.

My roommate Monk had partied hardy at the kegger and he was awakened from his stupor by the sights and sounds of a man in his underwear attacking his mattress with a Louisville Slugger.

"Tommy, Tommy. What's goin' on?", he inquired.

"There's someone under my bed! There's someone under my bed!", I insisted. By now the entire west wing of third floor Ireland was awake. Father Lavin, the priest who lived on the floor, was pounding on our door, wondering what in the blazes was going on.

"Tommy, Tommy. You're having a nightmare", Monk tried to calm me. "Tommy, wake up, man. It's just a nightmare."

By the time we let Father Lavin in, I was still convinced that someone had been under my bed. It never dawned on me that no living being could survive all of the dust under my bed. As I told my story to Father Lavin, many of my dormmates had formed an audience.

I finally realized that my arm had fallen asleep. That's why I hadn't been able to feel my own hand when I touched it with my other hand.

Even after we'd all gone back to bed, I had a tough time convincing myself that I hadn't had an uninvited guest. I had no trouble convincing myself that I'd been quite a spectacle.

When I woke the next morning, I knew this would be the talk of the dorm and the college cafeteria. I knew my episode of the night before was going to make great fodder for breakfast conversation, maybe also lunch and dinner. I was always quick to make light of my buddies' misgivings. Now it was my turn in the barrel.

I thought about skipping breakfast that day, but I decided instead to face this tomfoolery head-on. Plus, the alcohol from the night before had left me with a mild case of cotton mouth. I was hungry and thirsty.

"Maybe I'm making a big deal out of nothing", I thought to myself as I walked with my breakfast tray to sit with a group of buddies in the cafeteria. No one had even mentioned this fiasco yet.

Then it started.

"Batter Up", said Willie. "Hey, Batter, Batter! Swing, Batter, Batter!"

"Nothing like a little late night batting practice, Symalla?"

"Hey, Babe. Babe Ruth! Heard you beat the shit out your mattress last night."

"Yeah, what were you trying to do? Tenderize it?"

"Hey, Symalla. I heard you had a visit from the Tooth Fairy last night."

My Boogeyman was apparently out of the closet.

Miss Sorensten

Miss Sorensten was mad at me again. She'd asked Willie Newman and I to move our desks into the hall. The desks had been moved as the rest of our fourth grade class watched in amusement. You would have thought that the class would get bored watching me move my desk into the hallway of St. Boniface Grade School. It had become a frequent occurrence. Some kids hauled around their books and school supplies in schoolbags or book bags . I hauled around my entire desk. It was my lot in life, I had decided.

Willie and I had been making noises. You know, the kind of noises a person might make after eating a heavy helping of baked beans. The kind of noises my mom said were OK to make with family, but never in front of company, never at the table, and certainly never in church. Our family was better than that, she said.

Willie and I had created a duet of sorts, as we made fart noises with our mouths. Each imitation was followed by a round of muffled laughter. The girls seated near us never saw the humor in our antics, but that didn't matter to Willie and I. A couple of budding comedians, we tried to one-up each other and then we tried to contain our hysteria. It was the laughter that finally indicted us.

"Thomas Symalla and William Newman", yelled Miss Sorensten. "Do you care to tell the rest of the class what's so funny?"

Willie and I looked at each other before looking at Miss Sorensten. Neither of us volunteered to let her and the class in on our private joke.

"Very well then, boys. If you don't want to be part of this class, you're going to have to move your desks into the hallway. And please hurry, boys. We have other students here who are anxious to learn and you have apparently decided that learning doesn't suit you. You've distracted the class enough. Move your desks and please don't scratch the floors. Mr. Kammermeier just waxed them over the Thanksgiving holiday. If you need help moving your desks, I'm sure some of the other boys will help you."

Allen Stommes rose quickly to help Willie move his desk to the doorway. Billy Kaufman and Mark Steil helped me move my desk to the other doorway, where we deposited it in the hallway, facing it away from the class as was required.

I'd done it again. This was why I had so many checkmarks on the behavior side of my report card, I told myself. Parent-teacher conferences were in a couple of weeks and I wondered if Miss Sorensten would meet with my mom in the classroom, or in the hallway, where I spent so much of my time. The night of parent-teacher conferences would be a night when I would volunteer to wash and wipe the family dinner dishes, I decided.

Only the year before, in third grade, the desks had been molded together in rows. I had thought it was neat when we got the new, bigger desks in fourth grade. Little did I know, that I would have to carry mine around wherever I went. It was an unwanted appendage.

I didn't think my exile from the classroom would be long. Father Alto would be there soon to teach catechism class and Miss Sorensten would probably allow Willie and I to move our desks back into the classroom before he began. Father Alto could deal with us while she retreated to the serenity of the teachers' lounge.

It was Wednesday and it was the second time that week that Miss Sorensten had yelled at me. The scene of Monday's crime was the cloakroom, where I slipped a big glob of green Jell-O into Joanie Peters' boot. As she was an object of my secret affection, I was bound and determined to make sure no one knew that I liked Joanie Peters and this was my way of doing so. When she slipped into her snow boots at the end of the day, she let out an "Eew" for all to hear. "Miss Sorensten, someone put goop in my boot", she exclaimed.

An unbelieving Miss Sorensten inspected the boot and proclaimed, "That's not goop. That's Jell-O!"

I was quick to admit the mischief, hoping it would disguise my secret crush. I wasn't sure if my plan would work, but I was quickly informed that I wouldn't be going home just yet. Miss Sorensten wanted to talk to me. She talked to me a lot during the school day. I didn't see why she needed to talk to me after school too.

It had been a premeditated act on my part. Just the night before, I'd asked my mom to pack an extra helping of Jell-O with my lunch. I really like the Jell-O with the pineapple slices in it, I told her. She was happy to fill a large plastic Oleo margarine container with Jell-O for my next day's lunch, never thinking that it would end up as lining in a girl's golashes.

Months before, at the start of school, I'd been an accessory in yet another hijinx designed to entertain the class at Miss Sorensten's expense.

Immediately after recess, Miss Sorensten had begun to tell us about the Boston Tea Party. In 1773, a group of American colonists dumped crates of tea belonging to the British East Indies Company into the Boston Harbor as a form of protest. As she stood by her desk, Miss Sorensten stopped frequently, trying to identify the source of what sounded like someone crumpling papers.

Fresh out of St. Cloud State Teacher's College, Miss Sorensten was the only lay teacher we'd had so far in grade school. Although she was no Miss Landers, like in the "Leave It to Beaver" show, Miss Sorensten was OK, I guess. Anyway it was nice to have a lady teacher whose legs and neck we could see. All of the other teachers were nuns who wore the black and white habits of the Sisters of St. Benedict.

As Miss Sorensten told us that the Boston Tea Party sparked the American Revolution, she stopped again. She had identified the source of the rustling papers. Stooping over to look in the paper-filled metal wastebasket beside her desk, Miss Sorensten was greeted by an adult garter snake who poked his head up through the waste paper. Miss Sorensten's body jerked backward and her face convulsed before she ran out of the room screaming.

Some of the boys in the classroom responded with nervous giggles, while all the girls and the boys who were not in on the caper looked on in amazement. In her haste to exit the classroom, Miss Sorensten had broken a heel. She was lucky she didn't hurt herself.

When we'd been playing near the parish house garden at recess, Mark Granson had discovered the snake. We decided to use the brown kraft bag I kept in the back pocket of my jeans for the next day's lunch to transport the harmless foot-long reptile to the classroom. (Yes, I was too cool to have a lunch pail. Instead, I toted my lunches in a brown paper bag that I sat on all day.) We'd nixed the initial idea of planting the snake in Miss Sorensten's desk drawer for fear that she might drop dead of a heart attack. Parent-teacher conferences would be no fun then.

We settled for the wastebasket, placing the snake there before Miss Sorensten returned from the teachers' lounge and before the other kids were summoned by the bell announcing the end of recess.

After running out of the room in terror, Miss Sorensten eventually got her bearings back. Determined not to be humiliated by a bunch of fourth graders gone wild, she limped back into the classroom, kerchief in hand. But even with all her determination, she got nowhere close to the metal wastebasket. With firm resolve, and using her front teeth to settle her quivering lower lip, she demanded the identities of the culprits.

Our lips were sealed. This crime was too heinous to admit. None of the girls who had normally earned brownie points by ratting on the boys had been aware of the prank, so they were also mum.

Mary Ellen Petrarski was the biggest brown-noser of them all. When Miss Sorensten couldn't get any of her students to fess up to the misbegotten mischief, she turned to her favorite snitch.

"Mary Ellen, do you know who did this?"

"I'm sorry, Miss Sorensten. I'm not sure who did it. I was jumping rope at recess. But it must have been one of the boys. Some of them were in a circle by the parish house garden and they looked like they were up to something, as they usually are. I'm not sure who it was, Miss Sorensten, but if I had to guess who did it, I'll bet it was Billy, Tom, or Mark. Those boys are always getting into trouble."

After it became obvious that none of us was going to admit to our wrongdoing, there was still the matter of the snake in the wastebasket. After fear of recrimination had waned, Mark Granson decided to try for some brownie points of his own.

Raising his hand, angel that he was, "Miss Sorensten, if you'd like, I can take the snake outside and release it."

"That would be good, Mark. That would be good."

"I'm always happy to be of service, Miss Sorensten."

The entire classroom transfixed, Mark proceeded to the front of the room, picked up the wastebasket, and headed for the door. As he was about to exit the classroom and return the slithering serpent to its natural habitat, Miss Sorensten had a parting question.

"Mark, how did you know that it was a snake in the waste-basket? I never said it was a snake."

"Um. Oh, gee. I'm not sure why I thought it was a snake, Miss Sorensten. I guess it's because you went running and screaming like it was a snake."

"Mark, go release the snake. You and I will talk later."

And About Humpty Dumpty

A friend of mine recently tried to explain why it's so difficult for him to trust people. "I grew up in Philadelphia, where nobody trusts anybody. People in Philadelphia believe Humpty Dumpty was pushed off the wall. It's not our nature to believe that he just took an accidental tumble."

I'm also an admitted skeptic. Skepticism is a trait that has sometimes caused me unnecessary anxiety, as you'll note from the story that follows.

Years ago, my parents and I traveled to Austria, Switzerland, and Germany for three weeks. They were in search of the perfect slab of schnitzel; I was in search of a stein of beer which was too big to handle.

We had opted not to take one of those organized trips, which meant that we didn't have hotel reservations awaiting us as we traveled from city to city.

We had purchased a Eurail pass which allowed us unlimited travel on Western Europe's efficient rail system. Our daily routine was to arrive in the city where we'd be staying by late afternoon. I'd then search out a hotel room while my parents stayed behind with our luggage.

Finding accommodations within walking distance of the train stations was normally an easy task. Sometimes I asked to see the room before renting; always I asked if the free continental breakfast included cold cuts and hard rolls.

Another friend of mine told a story of arriving in Paris with his wife. Arriving at a late hour without hotel reservations, they trudged from hotel to hotel, always to find that there were no vacancies. In desperation, my friend finally settled for a room that rented by the hour and which he suspected was a place of business for those who were practicing or supporting the world's oldest profession.

My friend still boasts that he may have been the only guy in the hotel who didn't have to pay his roommate for the company. His wife still claims that he owes her for the evening,

But my parents and I hadn't had any problems securing hotel accommodations, at least until we arrived in Salzburg, Austria, in the middle of our European trip. After a long day of travel, we were anxious to find a room, park our baggage, and enjoy a nice dinner. As my parents stayed behind at the train station, I visited hotel after hotel, only to find no vacancies because of a local music festival. What was it with the Austrians and their music festivals? When I'd run out of options, I headed back to the train station, disappointed at the prospect of having to board the train again and seek late night accommodations in another city.

Upon my return to the Salzburg train station, I found that my parents had been befriended by a husky fraulein named Theresa, who was explaining that she had a room for rent in the Austrian countryside.

Despite the lack of success I'd had in securing a hotel room for the night, the Doubting Thomas in me surfaced immediately as my parents introduced me to Theresa. "How much money?", I quizzed her.

"$27 U.S. dollars", she responded.

"$27 for the room or $27 for each person?", I continued the interrogation, realizing that even $27 per person was comparable to what we'd been paying for hotels.

"$27 for da room. Das gut?"

"Yah, das gut", I responded. "But how do we get back to the city in the morning?"

"I get you der, I get you der", Theresa assured us.

I looked at my parents and they both gave me a what-else-can-we-do, it's-up-to-you shrug.

"OK. We will take the room", I told Theresa. "But how will we get there?"

"Das gut!", exclaimed Theresa. "My Frederick, he pick you up in 20 minutes and take you to da room in da country. He will drive a red Volkswagen. He meet you here. Please wait. Das gut?"

"Yah, das gut, I suppose."

Reluctantly, we nodded, as Theresa marched away. What had we gotten ourselves into, I wondered, recalling nightmarish tales about dumb, trusting Americans who had been victimized by their own naivete' in travels to foreign lands. I envisioned the headlines in an upcoming edition of *USA Today*, when news of my self-inflicted demise was announced to all. "Stupid American and His Parents Robbed and Left to Die in Austrian

Countryside"…or "American Business Owner and His Trusting Parents Victimized by Austrian Room Scam. What In the World Were Those Dopes Thinking?"

Despite our worst thoughts, my parents and I agreed to trust Theresa and her Frederick.

Frederick arrived promptly and when he opened the trunk to his red VW, I was somewhat surprised that he didn't pull out his Luger, point it at us, and motion for us to climb into the trunk. Instead, he asked us to place our luggage there. We were relieved to do so.

Expecting a drive to the foothills of the mountains, where we would be bound, robbed, shot, and left to die a slow, excruciating death, we were delightfully surprised when we arrived at a farmhouse in the country where we would stay the night. Frederick introduced us to an elderly woman named Edith, who had been widowed by the war and who let rooms and raised honeybees to support herself.

Our room was comfortable and cozy. We raved about the thickness of the down comforter and laughed at the sight of the piss pot under the bed. The proprietor's hospitality was warm and welcome. We enjoyed the Austrian countryside. We walked about a mile along a gravel road to the small town of Hallwang and had a nice dinner in a small restaurant. No one there spoke English, but they were happy to try.

When we returned to the train station the next day, we spotted Theresa, who we now knew as a legitimate recruiting agent for various persons who rented rooms in the country to travelers. Now that we'd lived to see another day, and paid only $27 in lodging to do so, Theresa was our friend and we went to thank her. She was in the middle of trying to convince a very non-trusting New York couple to rent one of her rooms in the countryside. These New Yorkers were experiencing the same apprehension we had felt the day before.

"Are you sure this is safe?", the man from New York asked us.

"Oh, sure. No problem. Nothing to worry about", we responded.

Reminded once again that Humpty Dumpty probably wasn't pushed off the wall.

Old Man Rasner

Whenever we couldn't round up enough players for a game in the converted cornfield by Vogt's, Wally Westrum and I would play one-on-one baseball.

The Symalla backyard was Metropolitan Stadium, and I was the Minnesota Twins with Harmon Killebrew, Bob Allison, Jimmy Hall, Earl Battey, and Tony Oliva. The Westrum driveway was Wrigley Field, and Wally was the Chicago Cubs with Ernie Banks, Billy Williams, Ron Santo, Randy Hundley, and George Altman.

Most of our games were played at the Met, where two large elm trees served as first and third base and a large post from the white picket fence that separated us from our neighbors served as second base. The same white fence was the homerun fence, so if we hit a fly ball anywhere over second base, it was a homerun. If we hit a fly ball through the window of my sisters' bedroom, it was a run home.

In the games between Wally and I, the Twins always won. Wally wasn't the baseball player I was, but he loved to play and he always played hard. The constant losing never seemed to bother him. Someday, he believed, the Cubs would finally win.

My mom had grown weary of the damage we were inflicting on my dad's finely manicured lawn. When she suggested to my dad that Met Stadium become unavailable for future baseball games, he was quick to remind her that they were raising kids, not grass.

Using cracked softball bats held together with medical tape and nails, and baseballs with few remaining stitches, Wally and I would often play for hours.

Our games were delayed however, when one of us hit a foul ball into Old Man Rasner's garden. Old Man Rasner was meticulous about his garden and in his failing voice, he had made it clear that he didn't want anybody in there trampling his beans, strawberries, or cucumbers. Because he didn't like kids, he was never willing to retrieve the balls which had invaded his garden.

When Old Man Rasner was in the house or at the Side Bar for his daily afternoon of euchre, we'd be able to reclaim our foul balls from his garden. We were always careful not to step on any of his plants. Grandpa Symalla had a big garden and he had taught me to respect plants , flowers, and the time people put into their gardens.

But most of the time, Old Man Rasner was outside, sitting in the white metal lawn chair that overlooked his precious garden. There was irony in the fact that he'd listen to every Twins baseball game on his transistor radio from his white metal throne.

Even though Old Man Rasner and I had a mutual love for the Twins, we never shared it with each other. I was a kid and he hated kids. He didn't see any reason for kids to exist. That's all there was to it.

Once, when we were retrieving a ball from Old Man Rasner's pickle patch, he sneaked up on us and doused us with water from his garden hose. Another time, he surprised us and chased us, waving his wooden cane as his faltering voice warned us to stay out of his garden. Even though we knew he couldn't catch us, we never retrieved our baseballs when Old Man Rasner was watching his garden grow. To a pair of 10-year-old boys, there was something creepy about being chased by a crabby old man.

In school, Wally and I had both liked the story of Hansel and Gretel, where an old witch locked a young boy in her oven. We liked the story because it gave us the heebie jeebies.

When we were trying to scare each other with nighttime stories, Wally and I had conjured up thoughts of our own Grimm's Fairy Tale. Old Man Rasner would sneak up behind us while we were looking for our baseball in his strawberry patch. He'd use the crook of his wooden cane to capture Wally or I by the neck, and he'd haul one of us away while the other watched in horror. The boy who was dragged away would never be seen again.

The surviving boy, Wally or I, depending on who was telling the story, would later figure out what happened to his playmate when Old Man Rasner's garden sprouted baseball plants the following spring. Brand new horsehide baseballs would appear in a section of Old Man Rasner's garden the year after one of us had disappeared. Hanging from vines like all his fruits and vegetables. Old Man Rasner would sport a knowing smile whenever his neighbors would ask him how he was able to grow such beautiful baseballs. "It's the fertilizer", he'd say.

With Old Man Rasner's lush green garden, we weren't always able to find our baseballs, even when we were able to sneak into his garden. Over the course of the summer, dozens of baseballs had disappeared in his garden. Old Man Rasner spent hours in his garden. He was obviously finding these missing baseballs, but he would never return them. They were trophies to him, we decided. Reminders of how much he hated kids. We wondered where he kept his collection. Probably in his garage, we thought, but neither Wally nor I had the guts to find out.

My initial complaints to my mom about Mr. Rasner taking our baseballs fell upon deaf ears. "Well, just don't hit foul balls", she offered the obvious solution. Mom was a baseball fan. She knew that foul balls were an inevitable part of baseball.

"We try not to, Mom. But sometimes it just happens."

"I know. And Mr. Rasner shouldn't be taking your baseballs. Maybe I'll see if your father will talk to him."

On a day soon after, when a lot of the neighbor kids had been hauled off on family vacations, Wally and I decided we'd pass the afternoon with a game of one-on-one. We had only one tattered baseball between us. The summer had taken its toll on our meager supply of baseballs.

"Maybe we should play in your driveway", I suggested to Wally. "We've only got one baseball left and Old Man Rasner is out in his yard sitting in his chair."

"Naw, we can't play at my house. My mom yelled at me last time we played. She said we put ball marks on the new aluminum siding. Let's play in your backyard. I'll be careful not to hit a foul ball."

Two pitches into what was supposed to be an afternoon's entertainment and a doubleheader, Wally hit a foul ball over the short chicken wire fence that separated our yard from Old Man Rasner's garden.

"Aw, geez, what do we do now?", asked Wally.

We weren't sure if Old Man Rasner had seen the foul ball go into his garden. He stared straight ahead as he always did. Either way, it didn't matter. Game over, we decided.

When Wally and I walked into our house, Mom was ironing Dad's shirts.

"Mom, what can we do?", I asked for ideas on how Wally and I could adjust our plans as I grabbed a popsicle for each of us.

"I thought you boys were going to play baseball? It's a beautiful day to be outside."

"We were playing baseball, but we hit our last baseball into Mr. Rasner's garden. I'll need to mow the lawn two more times before I have enough money to buy another baseball."

"You seem to be spending all of your allowance money on baseballs."

"I know, but Mr. Rasner keeps taking them. I might just as well have Dad give my allowance money directly to Mr. Rasner."

My mom turned off the iron. "Boys, I've had enough of this. I'm going to put an end to this once and for all."

She stormed out of the house. Wally and I watched from the kitchen window as Mom had an animated conversation with Old Man Rasner. But we weren't sure it was a conversation, because my mom did all the talking.

"Wow. Looks like your mom is really telling him off", Wally expressed newfound admiration for my mom.

I smiled in agreement.

Within minutes, Old Man Rasner rose from his chair, acknowledging my mom's resolve. He grabbed his cane from the arm of his chair. As he reluctantly stutter-stepped his way to the garage, my mom watched with hands on hips. Her dander was up. Old Man Rasner's dauber was down. He didn't have a chance in this one.

When he reappeared, he was carrying a wooden peach crate full of baseballs. Sheepishly, he handed them over to my mom.

Wally and I ducked from the kitchen window before our side door opened. We didn't want Mom to know that we'd watched the entire encounter.

We were back in the living room by the time Mom returned with the stash of baseballs. She was still steaming, so we didn't say a thing.

Finally, as she laid the Wagon Wheel peach crate on the kitchen table, she said, "Here are your baseballs, boys. Play all the baseball you want. But don't hit foul balls. And if you do, please be careful not to trample Mr. Rasner's garden."

We decided our two-pitch baseball game had been long enough for that day.

"I think Wally and I are going to walk down to Zastrow's Bridge to see if anyone is catching any fish. We'll be back in time for dinner. And thanks a lot, Mom."

Signals Missed

As my car made the familiar trek from Humperdink, Hornblower, and Witts bar and restaurant to my Richardson, Texas condo, I took some satisfaction from the knowledge that Marissa Patterson's interest in me had been confirmed. If I had only known earlier, maybe I could have done something about it.

Women are complex creatures, I admitted. Much too complicated for a simpleton like me. I'd never even been close to figuring them out. But then again, I'd never been good at reading signals, from women or men.

I first realized this shortcoming in eighth grade. As a kid who lived and breathed baseball since second grade, I'd begun to wonder if my dreams of being a major league baseball player were about to be doused by my inability to identify and hit a curveball. With the way I was hitting, I was afraid that I'd soon have to set my sights on another grownup profession. Instead of my parents and sisters being able to watch me perform as a second baseman at Metropolitan Stadium or Wrigley Field, they'd have to watch me board a Burlington Northern boxcar, as I embarked upon my second preference for a profession, the life of a hobo.

I was so preoccupied with my waning batting average that I didn't even pay attention to the pre-game signals assigned by Mr. Rogan, our eighth grade coach and also the head coach for the St. Boniface High School team.

Before each game, Mr. Rogan carefully outlined the signals we'd use for that day's game. The tug of his right ear lobe called for a bunt. An index finger to the tip of his nose called for a steal. The palm of his hand across his cheek called for a hit-and-run, or as far as I was concerned, it might as well have meant that Mr. Rogan had a smooth shave that morning.

I was in the middle of another slump and if I didn't break out of it soon, I'd be riding the pine, gathering splinters. If I ever reached base, I'd worry about the signals then.

In a game against Albany, I was again anchoring the bottom of the batting order when I stuck out my bat and blooped a leadoff single to right field.

Mr. Rogan applauded my good fortune from the third base coaching box. Before the next hitter, Mark Steil, stepped into the batter's box, Mr. Rogan tugged at his right ear. I never saw the sign, maybe because I was waiting for a parade to commemorate my third hit in the past 21 at-bats.

When Mark Steil dropped an adequate bunt down the third baseline, I was late in getting off the first base bag and the pitcher threw me out at second.

"Symalla, what were you doing?", shouted Mr. Rogan, as I dusted myself off from a futile slide designed to disguise my gaffe. When I went by him to get to the dugout, Mr. Rogan stopped me, patted my helmet and yelled, "Hello. Earth to

Symalla. Anybody in there? Earth to Symalla. Didn't you see me give the bunt sign?"

Mr. Rogan was a very good baseball coach. He knew more about baseball than anyone I knew. "Sorry, coach. I must have missed it. I thought he was going to hit away."

"Go sit down, Symalla, and get your head in the game. That's the third sign you guys have missed today. What's wrong with you guys? Do I have to wear a sandwich board telling you guys what to do?"

"Sorry again, Mr. Rogan. If I ever get on base again, I'll be sure to pay more attention to your signs." Head down, I trotted off the field, my bloop single already a distant memory.

I didn't know then that this missed signal at the Cold Spring Municipal Baseball Park would be a precursor of things to come. Looking back, that sandwich board idea wasn't half bad.

Eleven years later, my baseball days were over and my fallback plan of being a hobo was nixed by my parents when they pointed out that "our family doesn't have hobos". I'd decided to use my college degree to obtain gainful employment as a public relations associate at International Dairy Queen, corporate headquarters for more than 4,300 Dairy Queen and Dairy Queen/Brazier stores.

In the two years since college, a long commute to work had finally convinced me to move to an apartment in the suburbs of Minneapolis, away from most of my remaining college buddies.

Living alone in Bloomington, I missed the captive companionship of a bunch of guys living in an apartment. It would be nice if I had someone to play with, I thought.

I'd made friends quickly in my first job after college. Fortunately, IDQ hired a lot of young kids fresh out of college, and there were plenty of people for me to run with after work. For the most part, we worked hard and played hard as many of us eased into the transition from high school or college to real life.

Jillian McKenzie was among the people I met in my new job. JillyMac was also a P.R. associate, she was two months my elder, and our desks sat less than 10 feet from each other in a B.C. (before cubicles) era.

JillyMac and I had quickly become friends. With an unparalleled zest for life and a golden personality, Jilly was a lot of fun to be around. She loved almost all sports, and she could drink beer and tell dirty jokes with the best of us.

Jilly had an active social life from the time I first met her. My P.R. associates and I would get to work early Monday mornings to hear her weekend recaps. Her disastrous dating life was better than any soap opera and her life was an open book. JillyMac was a self-proclaimed bum magnet, which probably explains why I liked her and also relates back to the whole hobo thing.

Jilly and I had been among a group of eight people from work who had Minnesota Vikings season tickets. We enjoyed our time at the Vikes games immensely and I eventually admitted to myself that I enjoyed going to games with her more than I would have enjoyed going with any of my guy friends. And it wasn't just because she smelled better.

After the football season was over, Jilly and I took our love of sports to another level when we agreed to share University of Minnesota basketball season tickets. When we decided to get the tickets together, Jilly confessed that her knowledge of basketball paled in comparison to her knowledge of football and baseball.

She told me she'd cease and desist if her questions were too frequent or too stupid. As a self-proclaimed hoops guru who normally wouldn't want to watch a basketball game in the presence of someone who didn't know its ins and outs, I braced myself for what I might have been getting into. But I also agreed to take on my eager student. At worst, I thought to myself, the company would be good.

But I quickly discovered that my pupil's interest was sincere. She was a quick study and it wasn't long before she knew the difference between a man-to-man defense and a zone defense. I also quickly realized that it wasn't just about the basketball. Sometimes, she'd ask my opinion about the guys she'd been dating, some of whom I knew, some of whom I didn't.

"I'm afraid I can't help you with that, Jilly. Basketball, I can help you learn. But love and dating, you're asking the wrong person. You're on your own with that one, Toots."

Into the second half of the season on a Saturday night when our Golden Gophers were hosting Bobby Knight's Indiana Hoosiers, Jilly and I agreed that I'd arrive at her South Minneapolis duplex a couple of hours before tip-off. This was earlier than I normally picked her up, but it was a weekend and we'd agreed to make time for beers and appetizers before we headed to Williams Arena.

The pre-game primer was fun. Not that I would have expected anything else from JillyMac. The game was a good one. Even though the Gophers lost, JillyMac and I enjoyed the outing. We laughed, we cheered, we agonized over the hometown team's inability to make free throws, and we agreed that they'd have to play better to beat Purdue on Monday.

When the game was over, we made the short shuttle back to Jilly's place, where I was prepared to drop her off as I usually did. She'd been unusually quiet during the ride to her duplex, but I figured she was emotionally drained after a tough Gopher loss. She took the losses much harder than I did.

"You want to come in for a beer, Symalla?", she announced as I was about to tell her how much I'd enjoyed the game and the company. "Come on. It's early yet. I have a refrigerator full of beer and there's no school tomorrow, Bucko."

"A refrigerator full of beer, you say? Hmm. Hmm. Oh, what the hell. Twist my arm. I guess I am feeling really thirsty all of a sudden. Will it be OK if I make a pig out myself."

"Feel free to drink yourself silly, Porky. I'll pour your beer in a trough if you like it better that way."

Over the next couple hours, Pablo Cruz, Melissa Manchester, and Jerry Jeff Walker performed on JillyMac's stereo, as we worked on her ample stash of beer and traded stories.

Into her second beer, it occurred to me that Jilly seemed different that night. More serious, I thought. Other than that, I couldn't pinpoint what was different about her, but the prospect of another Pabst and the chance to continue to hear myself talk allowed me to dismiss my instincts.

Into my third beer, sitting with Jilly on her couch, I thought maybe she was looking at me different. I was definitely looking at her different, but the effects of alcohol had misled me more often than not. As I looked into her eyes, the bravado from the beer was still prompting me to make a move. But, I remembered her telling me earlier that evening about the guy she'd been dating. He was really nice, she said.

The fear of an alcohol-induced faux pas and the fear of ruining my best platonic relationship held me back. I quickly finished my beer and declared that it was time to hit the road. I had a big tennis match at the health club in the morning.

I retrieved my tennis shoes from the vestibule and pulled them on. Surprised at my sudden decision to call it a night, Jilly walked me to the door, where she gave me an effortless hug.

"Thanks for the beer, Toots."

"See you Monday, Roscoe", she smiled a reluctant smile. As Harry Chapin said in a song, it was a sad smile just the same. "I enjoyed the game, Symalla."

On the drive home, I replayed what had gone on. After some consternation, I applauded myself for my inaction, but I berated myself for almost screwing up one of the best friendships I had. "Goddamn, Symalla. What were you thinking? You need to start thinking with your head instead of with lower parts of your anatomy. You were almost willing to risk one of your best friendships for a one-time roll in the hay. What's wrong with you? You're lucky you left when you did. You could have made an ass of yourself. Didn't you hear her say that she was dating someone she liked?"

I took my own scolding like a man, convinced that I had misread the situation, convinced that I had made the right decision in aborting the evening. Man, I was glad I didn't make a move. With adjacent desks at the office, a dalliance of this sort would have certainly made for an uncomfortable Monday morning.

After assuring myself Sunday that my Saturday night inertia had been the right thing to do, I was at peace with myself by the time I arrived at my desk Monday morning. I was relieved not to have to worry about the awkwardness of an intimate encounter with a co-worker and my best female friend.

Jilly wasn't at her desk, but the Minneapolis Tribune there indicated that she was somewhere in the office. She must have gone to the coffee room, I thought. Whenever she got back to her desk, we'd enjoy our usual banter before we got into our work mode.

As I laid down my vinyl portfolio on my metal desk, I immediately noticed a sealed envelope resting on the only uncluttered area of my notoriously messy desktop. The non-posted envelope addressed to "Tom" quickly became the first order of the day. My morning coffee would have to wait.

Using my scissors to slit open the mysterious envelope, I found a banded bundle of Gopher basketball tickets. The tickets were enclosed inside a note which read:

Tom,

I'm sorry that I won't be able to go to any of the re-maining Gopher games.

I'm sorry to do this on such short notice and I hope you'll be able to find someone who enjoys going to the games with you as much as I did.

I can't tell you now why I can't go to these games with you, but I hope to tell you someday.

Your friend,

Jilly

Marissa Patterson.

I met her at a Happy Hour at Humperdink's on Greenville Avenue in Dallas. It was a Friday night gathering of thirty-somethings who worked for or had ties to my old restaurant company.

I hadn't met Marissa Patterson before. Surprisingly, because we'd worked for the same company, though at different times, I'd never even heard of her. Like me, she maintained friends from her stint at the old company.

As two of the last three people to arrive at the almost-weekly end-of-the-week Happy Hour, Marissa and I were forced to stand in the background, while most of the others gathered were seated in one of the large semi-circular booths or stools parked at the end of the booth. We'd grab chairs as soon as someone at the other tables relinquished his or her watering post.

Distanced from the main conversation, Marissa and I quickly introduced ourselves and initiated our own conversation. The conversation flowed easily and I enjoyed meeting someone new to our group of Happy Hour regulars. I immediately identified Marissa as someone who was both attractive and intelligent, with a nice sense of humor. She was a welcome relief after a long week of work.

We weren't far into our getting-to-know-all-about-you conversation when Marissa proudly pronounced that she'd given up dating months ago and she was happy with her decision. Where did that come from, I wondered? Her pronouncement wasn't in response to anything I'd said. It was without a segue. We'd been talking about TV shows before she made the statement. Either way, I got the message that Marissa Patterson was comfortable with her decision to remove herself from the dating pool. I had done the same, I noted, but it wasn't a conscious decision.

I didn't know Marissa well enough to feel either way about her declaration, but I took her statement at face value. My only hopes were to have a good conversation, since no one else appeared to be immediately available for the "Honey, I'm home" recap of a long week.

As the conversation continued, Marissa and I discovered that we had a lot in common. We'd both worked for the same company at different times. We had mutual acquaintances. We were both from the Midwest. She from Wisconsin, me from Minnesota. She was a passionate baseball fan, which automatically bumped her up a couple of notches on my compatibility scale. Married, then divorced, she noted that she had donated her basement to her ex-husband as a place to live until he could get on his feet financially.

"I didn't know houses in Dallas had basements", I quipped. "Is he free to roam around the basement or is he chained to the stairwell? Is there a dog food bowl near the bottom of the steps with his name on it? Sounds like a sex slave situation to me. Who needs a date when you can keep a sex slave in the basement? I'd do the same thing if I had a basement in my condo, and if I could ever find anyone who would exchange illicit sex for room and board. Sounds like you got it going on, lady."

Marissa laughed. "It's not like that at all. Well, maybe the doggie bowl part is true, but I don't have his name on it."

Our long conversation went quickly. The Happy Hour gathering of 14 people had dwindled to eight and some of the group initiated an idea to move down Greenville Avenue to Gershwin's, the hot new dining spot.

Cindy Klaassen sought commitments. "Marissa, are you up for dinner at Gershwin's?" Marissa looked at me. Then Cindy asked, "Symalla, are you in?"

"I'm in. I'm hungry as a horse. As a matter of fact, if they have horse on the menu, that's what I'm having. You're not a member of PETA, are you, Marissa?"

Marissa and I drove separate cars to Gershwin's, less than three miles down the road. Not quite sure where it was, she agreed to follow me, and when we arrived, we walked from the parking lot to the main entrance of the restaurant.

Trying not to be oblivious to other members of the dinner party, Marissa and I continued our conversation and, at least in my opinion, it never grew stale.

When the dinner at Gershwin's ended that night, we all said goodbye, see you at the next Happy Hour, and I walked Marissa to her car, which was next to mine.

"Marissa, I really enjoyed meeting you. I had a great time." We hugged goodbye and I cautioned her to drive safely. "Maybe I'll see you at one of the next Happy Hours."

In the short trip home that night, all I could think about was Marissa. If only she was dating, I thought, I'd make a run at her. Or in my case, history considered, I'd at least make a walk at her. Before I arrived at my condo, I'd resolved my feelings. She's not into dating. It is what it is, I guess. I didn't think about it again.

Six days had passed when my assistant Pam beeped in on my telephone intercom and asked me if I knew a Marissa Patterson. She was on the phone. Did I want to talk to her?

"Sure, I'll talk to Marissa", picking up the phone. "Marissa Patterson. How are you, my dear? It's good to hear from you again. What's up?"

"Hey, Symalla. I got your phone number from Barb. Am I catching you at a bad time? If so, I can call you back. If not, do you have time to give me a phone number?"

"So you want my phone number? I'm flattered. But, if I'm not mistaken, you got me at this number, didn't you?"

She knew I was kidding. "No, not your number, silly. You mentioned that you speak to Johnna every once in a while. Do you have her number? I'd like to touch base."

"Sure, let me grab my Rolodex. While I'm doing that, let me tell you again how much I enjoyed meeting you the other night. I enjoyed the conversation, and despite the beers, I remember most of it. And I must admit that I was surprised that you were willing to share your dirty mashed potatoes with someone you just met."

"Well, it probably would have been better if you hadn't used your hands to eat the mashed potatoes, but we can work on that. I also enjoyed the evening."

"Hey, I'm sorry about the polyester pants. If I had known I'd be meeting someone new at Happy Hour, I'd at least have worn a pair of wool or cotton slacks."

"Nothing wrong with shiny pants, Symalla. If the power had gone out in the restaurant, at least we wouldn't have needed candles at our table. Hey, I'm sorry about being short on cash. Thanks for paying for my dinner. I hadn't realized that I'd depleted the huge wad of money that I normally carry around in my fake designer purse."

"No apologies necessary, Miss Patterson. I didn't mind paying for your dinner. After all, it was either that or watch you wash dishes in the kitchen. I've never enjoyed watching people wash dishes, including myself. Although I'll bet that you'd have been a big hit with the guys in the dishroom. Probably would have been the hottest tamale they had worked with in quite some time."

"Well, I'd like to pay you back."

"Fine. Just send a cashier's check or a money order to my attention at 9225 Markville Avenue, Dallas, Texas 75214."

"No, seriously, I'd like to pay you back. Do you like oysters? Oysters on the half shell?"

"I love oysters."

"I hear they are excellent aphrodisiacs", she commented.

"Pam", I yelled into the other room. "What's an aphrodisiac?" Pam was on the other line.

"How about we go to the Greenville Avenue Country Club Friday and get us some of those afferdeeziaks?"

I hesitated, but not for the reasons she thought. "I have nothing against natural stimulants, but to be honest with you, I normally don't need much more than a hot blonde and a couple of Heinekens. You wouldn't know where I can get a hot blonde, would you?"

"Or, if you'd like, Symalla, I'll make dinner for you at my place. We'll have to give money to my ex to get him out of the house for the night. Either that or I'll tighten his leash. I make a mean chicken cacciatore. What do you think?"

"Sounds great, but I leave for a trade show in Chicago tomorrow. We're exhibiting at the national restaurant show."

Just then, Pam beeped in on the intercom. "Tom, Ethan is on line 3. He says he needs to talk to you before he goes into his meeting."

"Tell him I'll be with him in a minute."

"Marissa, did you hear that? I have a customer on the other line who needs some pricing before he goes into a meeting. I have to let you go. But, wait, let me give you Johnna's number before you go. Got a pen?"

"Yeah, go ahead."

"Let's see. Here it is. 817/862-2224."

"817/862-2224. Thanks, Symalla. I'll let you go. Have a nice trip to Chicago."

We never talked again. I didn't realize until later that her main reason for the phone call may have not been to get Johnna's number. If it had been any more obvious, it would have hit me on the head, but it took me a while to figure it out.

Months later at another after-work get-together, mutual friend Barb Lewis asked, "Tom, do you remember Marissa Patterson?"

"Yeah, I remember Marissa. We only met once, but I really enjoyed talking to her. She seems really nice. Why are you asking?"

"Well, she was really interested in you? Did you know?"

"You know, I finally figured that out, but it took me a while. When we first met, she made it crystal clear that she wasn't in the dating mode and I wasn't even asking. I took her at her word. But then she called me about a week after we met and I got the feeling she was interested. So was I, actually, but I was leaving for Chicago the next day and then things got really busy when I got back. I guess there were some signals that I didn't pick up until later or until I thought it was too late."

"Well, I just thought you'd like to know."

"Next time you talk to her, please let her know I felt the same way. Now that I think about it, I really should have picked up on it. Anyway, tell her I'm sorry. Tell her I'm really sorry."

I was moving back to Minnesota in five days.

Visiting Day

It was Visiting Day at St. Boniface Grade School. As part of Sister Arlene's second grade class, I'd received specific instructions to be on my best behavior…or else.

In the days before housewives were called homemakers, most moms, including mine, were in charge of raising the kids. It was an era when very few moms worked outside the home. Dads, on the other hand, were the designated breadwinners. With a bulk of the childraising responsibilities bestowed on mothers, most dads played a supplementary role in the raising of their kids.

In our household, my dad was assigned all of the outside stuff. Keep the garage clean, keep the lawn mowed, keep the sidewalks shoveled, keep the garden weeded, keep the cars running. As soon as I was old enough, he promptly reassigned most of these duties to me in return for a small stipend. However, one of the duties he could not reassign was his responsibility to administer discipline to his children. Unfortunately, this was almost a full-time job in my family. My dad played a very active role in my rearing. His belt and my rear spent some time together.

When Father's Day rolled around every year, a new belt for my dad was never a gift consideration. A clip-on tie would be just fine.

Every time my mom yelled, "Wait until your father gets home", we knew my dad would be instructed to discipline us when he got home that evening.

So with mother and father roles as they were in those days, it was almost all moms and no dads who attended Visiting Day at St. Boniface Grade School. Throughout the school day, our classroom played host to an ongoing influx of mothers, who would watch us from the back of the classroom as we got some education.

As I was the oldest child in our household, my mom still wasn't quite sure what Visiting Day was all about. I assured her that it was no big deal and that only a few of the other moms would attend, even though I knew that just about every kid's mom would probably attend. With a young daughter at home and another on the way, my mom decided not to attend our annual elementary school showcase. I was glad to know that Sister Arlene wouldn't be able to tell my mom about some of my misadventures. The doctor had said that Mom wasn't supposed to have a lot of stress when she was pregnant and finding out about my behavior at school was sure to give her more stress than she wanted.

I sat in the front of the classroom, because I was one of the shortest kids in class and because I couldn't sit still. It was because I couldn't sit still that Sister Arlene never took a liking to me. When she wasn't whacking me with her wooden blackboard pointer, she was giving me unusually difficult words in our weekly spelling bees. Asked to spell "juvenile delinquent", "testosterone", and "psychopath", it's no wonder I could never beat Mary Arnold or Patty Eisenzimmer to become class spelling champ.

I was unusually antsy on Visiting Day. It must have been all the excitement. Looking to the back of the room, I smiled and waved at Mrs. Virant and Mrs. Steil, a couple of the ladies who were in my mom's bridge club. I wasn't sure how bridge was played, but it didn't look near as fun as Slapjack. From what I could tell, my mom's card club was more of a social thing, in which the ladies would sample each other's desserts, tell each other how nice their houses looked, and throw in a few tidbits about their hubbies and kids.

As Visiting Day progressed and the back of our classroom filled with moms, I became a human jack-in-the-box. Getting up time and time again, I walked around my desk. Sometimes I'd talk to Weezie Kuebelbeck, the girl behind me. Sometimes I'd look out the window to make sure the weather was nice enough to play softball at recess.

Sister Arlene, who was all too familiar with my antics, had publicly but politely encouraged me to remain in my seat while she taught mathematics. When my rambunctiousness continued, Sister Arlene implored me to please remain in my seat. She showed much more patience than she would have if all the moms weren't in the back of the room. When imploring didn't work, she tried scolding.

"Thomas Symalla. Please sit down and remain seated."

"Yes, Sister."

Still I couldn't sit still. It wasn't long before I was at it again. As I turned around to talk again to Weezie Kuebelbeck, Sister

Arlene halted her mathematics lesson and marched over to my desk, where I became an unsuspecting victim.

When Sister Arlene lifted me off the ground by my left ear, I let out a yelp that would have left a coonhound proud. To this day, I swear that my left ear is larger than my right; it'll be an easy target if I ever get in a dogfight. Although Sister Arlene wasn't very tall, she sure packed a punch. Left with a throbbing ear, I wondered why she waited until Visiting Day to show everyone that she'd be working on the pectoral muscles she kept hidden under that baggy black habit of hers.

I turned beet red when I realized immediately that news of this spectacle would find its way back to my mom at the next ladies' card club. And it did.

Confined to my room, as I always was when the ladies were there to play cards, I could see it in my mind as plain as day: Mom, sitting at the card table, enjoying a forkful of that wonderful Hershey pie that I'd never again enjoy. One of the ladies just happened to mention how eventful second grade Visiting Day had been. As the story was unveiled, Mom's face turned purple as she choked down her dessert.

"Tom? Whose Tom? My Tom? My Tom did that?"

"Oh, yes. Your Tom!" Even some of the ladies who didn't have kids in second grade had heard about my public admonishment.

"Tom? My Tom?" My mom continued to voice her disbelief.

As I inventoried my baseball cards in a spiral noteboook, I wished that the last of the card club ladies would never leave, for fear of the consequences which awaited me.

When the last lady had said her goodbyes, the words "Thomas Michael, get out here right now" summoned me from my room. Mom was livid. She was angry about my Visiting Day misbehavior. She was angry because I told her that none of the other mothers would be there. She was angry for me embarrassing her in front of her friends. She was angry because I hadn't told her about the incident. She was angry about being my mom. She was just plum angry.

I endured her lecture. Most of the times when I did something wrong, she'd chase me around the dining room table with the yellow flyswatter, but she was too angry for that. Without a word, I pretended to listen intently to everything she said. If I didn't pretend to be sorry, I'd be grounded forever. No more high school football or basketball games. No more playing "Starlight, Star Bright, Hope to See a Ghost Tonight" with the neighbors.

The diatribe was finally over when Mom warned me, "Just wait until your father gets home. We'll see what he has to say about all of this. Now, go to your room and stay there, young man. I don't want to see you or hear from you again until supper."

Future Visiting Days at St. Boniface Grade School were never the same. Not only did they become "standing room only" events for my class, I could always be sure that my mom would be there...for the whole day. And, if I couldn't sit still, the nuns were no longer my main concern.

No, Not Really

Rifle resting in my lap, head propped against the trunk of an old elm tree, I'd become way too comfortable. Yawns came more frequently as the lack of activity and the warmth of a mid-autumn afternoon lulled me into a state of semi-consciousness.

Less than an hour earlier, a loud bell had sounded the end of another school day. Instead of lingering with friends, I'd bolted from my sophomore art class to my locker, where a brown kraft grocery bag held my grubbies. Like a quickchange artist, I'd used a bathroom stall to get out of my school clothes and into my hunting grubs. Boots tied, I'd made a beeline to the school nurse's office, where my mom worked.

She'd agreed to turn over the keys to her '62 Chevy Impala in return for my promises to be careful and to be home in time for supper. She'd arranged a ride home with one of the other ladies. I tried not to appear impatient as she again vented her concerns about my hunting alone, a replay of our conversation the night before. As she pretended to look for her keys at the bottom of her purse, she was well aware that she had a captive audience.

Thankfully, Mr. Boettschen came into the office, the car keys magically appeared from her purse, and the remainder of her "be careful" lecture ended immediately. Before she could say,

"Hello, Fred", I was out the door of the school and into the rusty but trusty Chevy.

The patch of woods near Big Watab Lake was only about seven miles from school. I was anxious to get there, as the days were growing noticeably shorter. Also, this was the first time I'd been hunting by myself and I didn't want to wait to experience my independence.

My dad and I had hunted this area before and there had been some activity. I unloaded the .22 rifle from the trunk of the car and made the short trek into the leaf-crusted woods. The first frost had hit about 10 days ago and the leaves had been quick to abandon the trees that had hosted them for the past six months. In the process, lots of squirrels' nests had been exposed.

We'd tried hunting before the frost, but the squirrels had been well-camouflaged against the leaves of the trees. Although we'd always had some success, it had never been easy.

Now, with the leaves gone, it would be a lot easier to spot my targets.

I selected an area on the ground below a couple of ancient oak trees, home to four squirrels' nests. As the damp ground seeped into the seat of my blue jeans, I wished I would have brought something to sit on.

I'd learned from hunting with my dad that if I kept quiet, the squirrels would eventually resume their normal activities, which at this time of year, consisted mostly of gathering nuts, seeds, and other food for the winter.

Squirrels were always fat this time of year. I got the feeling that they often ate most of the stuff they were supposed to be gathering for the winter. Just like when Mom and my sisters made cookies, I thought. They'd eat the first batch of cookies while they were making the second batch. I stayed away from the kitchen during these mother-daughter activities, well aware of all the dirty dishes which would result from a round of baking. Well aware that I was one of the family's designated dishwashers.

But, from a distance, I always enjoyed the scuffles my sisters had over who got to lick out the frosting bowl. Because she was four years older, Barb usually had first dibs. But Mom had always made sure that Joan got her shot at the bowl. After all, she was the baby. After all, licking out the frosting bowl was one of the biggest perks of helping a mom make cookies.

When the squirrels' nests I'd parked myself below were void of any activity on this afternoon, my thoughts returned to the last time I'd gone squirrel hunting with my dad.

Again, there hadn't been a lot of action when we first arrived. My dad and I had selected outposts in different areas of the woods. We were within shouting distance of each other, but we were alone at our posts.

Groggy from boredom, my head had bobbed up and down as I tried to fend off an impending nap. My tug-of-war with consciousness had been interrupted when a brown four-legged creature wandered toward me. When he noticed me, he stopped and studied me as I acknowledged his presence.

"Here doggy, doggy", I whispered. "Here doggy, doggy."

Grabbing half of a baloney sandwich from my jacket pocket and extending my hand with a come-join-me offering, I had asked, "Are you hungry, boy? Here, boy. You look awfully skinny. What's wrong, boy? Haven't they been feeding you?"

I didn't know if my visitor liked baloney, but he was skinny enough that I thought he'd eat just about anything.

He had contemplated the sandwich for a moment, but never came closer before he continued into the woods.

When my dad and I met up again before we headed home that day, he asked me if I'd seen the wolf that had come through. "Oh, that was a wolf?", I asked. "Gee, I thought that was a stray dog", never admitting that I'd offered the thing my sandwich. Never admitting that I'd invited the thing to lunch. Never admitting that I would have tried to teach the thing some simple dog tricks when we were done with lunch. It was my version of Little Red Riding Hood, I guess. Except I wasn't wearing a red hood and carrying a wicker basket and the wolf wasn't wearing granny's nightgown. Maybe that's why I didn't recognize him.

As my mind continued to wander, I wondered if I'd ever get the chance to ask Allison Adams to the Homecoming Dance. When the school year had started, when she was still going out with Mitch McGowan, Alli and I had often been the first students to arrive in Miss Thyson's English class. While most of the students conversed in the halls, Alli and I had exchanged pleasantries in the classroom before the bell sounded and the other students filled the classroom.

Although our talks were always brief, I started to look forward to them and I admitted to myself that I had liked her ever since she was the first person to ask me to dance at our eighth grade dance. Despite my developing interest, none of this had mattered much anyway when she was going out with Mitch McGowan.

Much to my dismay, Mitch McGowan was a high school heartthrob. Tall and good-looking, with his Beatles haircut, his bad boy image, and his apparent alley cat charm, Mitch McGowan had the pick of the litter in our school. I never understood what all the fuss was about, but most of the girls in our class turned to mush when presented with the attentions of Mitch McGowan.

I never understood. Mitch wasn't bright. He didn't have much of a personality. He wasn't an athlete. He wasn't a scholar. He wasn't in a band. But chicks thought he was cool and that made him cool. It pissed me off that he was cool. And it pissed me off that he knew that he was cool.

In freshman year, Cheryl Hendricks had succumbed to His Coolness. Like a shark toying with his prey, Mitch chewed her up and spit her out within a matter of weeks. When he was done with her and when he got what he wanted, Mitch split and moved on to his next victim. Cheryl, her reputation sullied, went from one of the most popular girls in school to someone who was a step below a leper.

We had studied the leper colonies in our CCD classes. In the Middle Ages, lepers had been deported to remote areas or islands because people were afraid that the lepers were highly contagious.

Cheryl Hendricks had been relegated to her own high school island when she was dumped by Mitch McGowan. It didn't matter that she had a face like Sophia Loren, it didn't matter that she was sharp as a tack, it didn't matter that she was one of the nicest people in the school. Cheryl Hendricks had become one of Mitch McGowan's rejects and, as a result, she was destined to spend the rest of her high school days on the outside looking in. No one should have that kind of power, I decided, especially someone like Mitch McGowan.

But I was a hypocrite, I thought. I had cringed when Cheryl Hendricks had asked me to be her partner in Spanish class. Oh, I had agreed to be her partner, but I was disappointed to know that I had even hesitated. Disappointed to know that I had hesitated to study with someone who was pretty, smart, and nice.

Just three weeks ago, Mitch McGowan had proudly announced that he was done with Allison Adams. Continuing to build his hollow high school legacy, he had boasted that he got what he wanted from Allison and he would be moving on to newer, more challenging notches in his belt. Ardent admirers of the female variety were encouraged to inquire within.

I had been happy to learn that Alli was no longer with Mitch. She definitely deserved better. And I thought I was better. But I was also well aware that Alli's popularity would plummet as a result of the breakup. I had resigned myself to the condemnation I'd have to endure from some of my buddies who expected me to shun her like everyone else. The criticism wouldn't be fun, but hopefully it would be worth it.

Since the breakup, my friends Pat Benoit and Mike Loesch had told me that Alli was interested in me. I'd been delighted to hear of her interest, even though I'd faked nonchalance when they told me of her interest. Leper or not, I liked Allison Adams. Now, if I could just get the balls to ask her out.

I'd been getting to English class early for the past two weeks, in the hopes of reconnecting with Alli and then asking her out. It was the only class we had together and we weren't in any activities together, so I viewed pre-class small talk as my best opening for asking her to the Homecoming Dance. But she hadn't been early for class lately and I still hadn't had my chance. The breakup with Mitch had hit her hard, I'd heard.

If I was going to ask Allison to the dance, it would have to be before Miss Thyson's English class. I knew I couldn't call Alli. I hated talking on the phone. And besides, our only home phone was in the kitchen, where my two younger sisters always seemed to be lurking any time there was a phone conversation. With the perked-up ears of German shepherds, they'd relish the thought of their older brother asking a girl to the Homecoming Dance.

I'd never hear the end of it. All of the teasing they'd suffered at my expense would come back to bite me.

"Tommy and Alli sitting in a tree. K-I-S-S-I-N-G. First comes love, then comes marriage, then comes Tommy with a baby carriage."

Telegram. Telephone. Tell-A-Sister. There was no faster way to spread a message in any household.

I looked above at the quartet of nests. Still no squirrel activity. Where were they? Had I picked some empty nests to sit under?

I started to resume my siesta and my thoughts of Allison Adams when a rustling of nearby leaves and sticks encouraged my attention. A lone chipmunk was frolicking about 15 feet away. Darting in and around a large pine tree, stopping every now and then to make sure no one had discovered his zeal, the woods were his playground.

Frolicking, foraging, digging, darting. I watched intently as the playful critter stuffed his cheeks with seeds. If only my sister Barb was here, I thought. She loved chipmunks. She'd taken a liking to the cartoon character chipmunks: Alvin, Simon, and Theodore. She played their record on the phonograph over and over again until I hoped she would wear it out. But then again, I could never tell if she really liked these twangy songs or if she just liked to irritate me.

I held still watching the chipmunk until I got an itch on my nose. Moving slowly to rub my nose, I didn't want to chase away the afternoon's only entertainment. The brown and black striped critter noticed my movement, stopped in his tracks, and surveyed the situation. When he decided I was friend, not foe, he continued his scavenger hunt. He even acknowledged my presence by chattering "chuck-chuck-chuck, I know you're there."

I responded by clicking the roof of my mouth repeatedly. My new friend apparently understood my language and he crept closer, stopping frequently to study me. As he continued to frolic and forage only four feet away from my Red Wing boots, I could tell that he was no longer afraid of me. Curious, maybe. But not afraid.

The life of a chipmunk didn't seem all that bad, I thought to myself. No homework, no having to rake the yard, no having to agonize about whether you're ever going to get the chance to ask Allison Adams to the Homecoming Dance. Being a chipmunk probably wasn't very complicated, I decided.

My interest waning, I raised my rifle and blew the chipmunk to bits. The rifle sounded like a cap gun as it shattered the silence of the woods. Eventually, I got to my feet and walked the few steps to the pulsing chunk of fur that lay dying. When it finally lay still, I reached down and felt the warmth of my recent playmate. Just seconds ago, he'd been a living, breathing creature just like me. For whatever reason, I'd decided to become his executioner.

When I looked at what remained of this creature, I saw something that I hadn't known was in me. I saw something I didn't like.

There was still an hour remaining before I was due home for supper. Not feeling good about what I'd done, my day in the woods was over. I thought about pulling out my pocket knife and clipping the tail of my victim, but quickly realized that it wouldn't be a badge of honor. There was no honor involved.

When I arrived home from my first solo hunting trip, my sisters rushed out of the house to see if I'd shot any squirrels.

"Did you get any? Did you get any?", they asked.

"No. No luck today", I told them.

"Well, was it fun?", my sister Joan asked enthusiastically.

"No, not really."

16 Again

Nervous energy emanated from the driver's seat of my parked 2004 Jeep Grand Cherokee as I rehashed the circumstances that had led to my predicament.

Just yesterday, I'd finally opened the envelope from Geico. Weeks earlier, a la Kreskin or Carnac the Magnificent, I had held the unopened envelope to my forehead, had presumed that it contained an early insurance renewal statement, and without opening it, designated it for further aging on my cluttered cadenza.

When I finally got around to opening it, I found a personal note from a Geico underwriter. According to her, a routine records check showed that I did not have a valid Minnesota driver's license, and if I intended to maintain my insurance with them, I'd need to provide them with a driver's license number within 30 days. The memo was dated October 31, 2007. Because I'd assumed my own extrasensory perception and because it was now November 29, I had only two days to respond.

No problem. I'll just call them with my driver's license number. Yet another case of corporate bureaucracy and red tape. The insurance company has lost my driver's license information.

Retrieving my driver's license from the caverns of my wallet and scouring my desk for my reading glasses, I quickly scanned my driver's license for the expiration date area. I couldn't remember the last time I'd looked at my license. I didn't use it to cash personal checks and I hadn't been stopped by a police officer in more than a decade. Still scanning the license for the expiration date, I stopped at my photo, admiring a more abundant patch of hair on top of my head and noticing a beard that was brown instead of brown and grey.

"I'll be damned", I pronounced to myself upon finding that my driver's license had expired almost five years ago. "How in the hell did that happen?"

I resolved immediately to travel to the nearest Department of Motor Vehicles location. With only two days remaining before my insurance company dropped me like a hot potato, and with a meeting-filled agenda the following day, I wanted to renew my license yet that day.

I stood patiently in line at the Arden Hills DMV location. If and when I finally reached the front of the line, I'd turn in my completed application, take the vision test, pose for a facial photo, pay my renewal fee, and then be on my way with paperwork toward a renewed driver's license.

At the counter, the DMV lady quickly informed me that renewing my driver's license wasn't going to be the microwave process I thought it was going to be.

"Your license has been expired over four years."

"Yeah, I just realized that this morning when I got a note from my insurance company. That's why I'm here. I'd like to get legal again."

"Well, Thomas, since it's been over four years since your license expired, you're going to have to take the written exam and the road test again. "Did you take the road test when you were a teenager or did they use horses and buggies in those days?"

Her attempt at humor eluded me. "You're kidding me? I have to retake the tests? The written exam and the road test? Both of them?"

"Yes, Thomas. You'll have to take and pass both tests in order to get a license again. I'm sorry, but your old license is no longer valid", cutting off a corner of the license and tossing it into the trash receptacle below the counter.

"Will I be able to do that today? My insurance company is requesting that I get them license information by tomorrow. I'm normally more responsible than this."

"Well, if you'd like to take the written exam today, I can give you a new form to fill out and you can go stand in that line", she said, pointing to a seemingly endless line. "Or, if you'd like to study for the test, I can give you this manual and you can come back another time."

"What about the road test?"

"If you pass the written test, you'll be eligible to take your road test. However, I must tell you that you'll have to make an appointment for the road test and sometimes it takes two to three weeks before you'll be able to take the test."

"Is there any way I'll be able to take the road test today?"

"Well, you can ask them at the next station. Sometimes they'll let you wait in line without an appointment, and if someone doesn't show up for their test, they'll take someone who doesn't have an appointment. But it's hit or miss. It depends on how many people are in the no appointment line, and you could wait all day and not get in."

"That's good to know. I'll take my chances, I guess."

"OK then, Thomas. Take this clipboard, complete the form, and then you'll have to stand in line over there. When it's your turn, they'll seat you at one of the computer terminals. Good luck."

As I stood in line for my written exam, I wondered if I'd been too complacent in opting to take the test without studying. Sure, I'd been driving for almost 40 years now. Sure, I'd probably forgotten more about driving than most of the young whippersnappers who'd be taking the same test. But then again, maybe the optimum word was "forgotten". Maybe I had forgotten things that I'd need to know to pass my driver's test.

I thought about grabbing a driver's manual and heading back to my office for a quick cram session, but there wasn't time for that if I was going to have a shot at getting my license yet that day.

About an hour later, I was directed to an exam station, where a bevy of multiple choice questions awaited.

Although I didn't ace the written test, I settled for passing it. As far as I was concerned, this was a pass/fail test. Time was of the essence.

When the lady behind the counter informed me that I'd passed the written part of the test, I quickly inquired, "They told me in the other line that I might be able to take my road test today, if I'm willing to wait in the no appointment line. Will that be possible?"

"You can try. There's a drive-thru window outside the building. If you'll hand the paperwork to the person at the window, they'll be able to tell you if you'll be able to wait in the no appointment line."

"Thanks. You've been helpful."

Slip in hand, I headed to my car. It was already 11:30 and there were already a number of cars in the no appointment line. Computer stations and drive-thru windows at the DMV, I thought. We were indeed living in the 21st century, unlike the century when I had taken my last driver's test.

When I finally reached the drive-up window, I tendered a "Hi, how's it going?" to the guy in the Navy Seals cap. "I'd like to see if I can take my road test today. I don't have an appointment, but I understand that if I'm willing to wait, I might have a chance to take the test if someone doesn't show up?" I offered my paperwork.

Reaching for my paperwork, the guy in the window was quick to ask, "Are you accompanied by a licensed driver? You need to be accompanied by a licensed driver."

"Oh, I'm supposed to have a licensed driver with me? I didn't know that. I don't have one with me. Is that a problem?"

The man closed his window without responding. I wondered if he was going to summon a police officer. Would I get a ticket? Would they tow my car? Would I be promptly delivered to the hoosegow? After all, I was operating a motor vehicle without a license.

I kept waiting for the man behind the window to pick up a phone and call the authorities, but he continued to write. When he was finished, he opened his window and handed me a clipboard.

"Pull ahead into Lane 6 behind that grey car and wait for an examiner. I made a note on your sheet that you're not accompanied by a licensed driver, so, if you fail the test, you'll need to call someone. We won't allow you to leave the premises without a licensed driver."

"Thank you."

I pulled up as the third car in Lane 6. It was then that my mental scattershooting began.

Not only could I lose my insurance and then my leased car, but worse, I'd have to call two family members to come and pick me up because I needed to be accompanied by a licensed driver. Deservedly so, I'd then never hear the end of this from my family.

As I looked around, I quickly noted that all of the other persons taking the road tests were teenagers. Accompanied by parents or licensed friends, they celebrated with hugs and high fives upon passing their tests. Me, I was the only fat, balding guy with reading glasses who was older than all of the examiners. I could barely remember the exaltation of passing my driver's test as a 16-year-old.

I remembered the two road tests I'd taken in Paynesville. I'd been passing the first test with flying colors until I rolled through a stop sign. The examiner immediately informed me that I'd violated a law and I'd have to take the test again in another six weeks.

Determined to gain my independence, I showed up again, father in tow, in six weeks exact. This time the pressure was on, as none of the guys in school had needed to take the test three times to get their license. Maysie Schmitz had needed more than three times, but she couldn't drive her bike to school without crashing it into a tree.

Before the second test, I'd been unusually nervous. My nervousness manifested itself in the form of a gas problem.

When the examiner entered the passenger side of the family's '62 Chevy Impala, he was quick to comment. "Smells funny in here. What's that odor?", quickly rolling down his window.

I didn't want to tell him that I'd been farting up a storm, so I lied.

"I'm sorry about that, sir. My dad and I went duck hunting this past weekend and I guess those dead ducks smelled up the car some. We were going to put them in the trunk, but that's where my dog Blackie rides and we were afraid he was going to chew up the mallards, so we…"

"OK, let's proceed. Go to the parking lot exit and take a left at the stop sign, please."

Back inside my Jeep and 38 years older, I remembered vaguely the lady inside the building telling me that I'd have to pass an equipment test before I started. Equipment test? What does that mean? Immediately, I scavenged for the owner's manual that had buried itself under the oil change receipts in my glove compartment.

I'd had the Jeep for almost four years now and I realized that I still wasn't sure how the power locks worked. Every time a passenger tried to get in my locked car, they'd have to watch me fiddle and fidget with most of the buttons on my door and, by the time they were finally able to get in, the windows were down, the windshield wipers were on, and I was mumbling to myself that, "Someday, I'm going to have to figure out what all these buttons are for."

Well, today , the day of an emergency driver's test, was apparently someday. I scanned the owner's manual with purpose, determining how to use the automatic locks and locating my flashers. I honked my horn, flashed my flashers, and flicked my brights to make sure they were working. The kid in the car next to me looked at me like I was a real wingnut, flashing me a look that said, "Hey, Dude, what's up with the horn blowing? A little nervous about taking the test, are we?"

Just to make sure my power locks were working, I hopped out of my Jeep and checked to make sure the passenger door was unlocked. I wouldn't be having a road test if the examiner couldn't get into the front passenger seat. And it might be a bit much to ask him to walk along side the car while he tested me. I scuttled back into the driver's seat, where I promptly made sure my seat belt was fastened.

Parallel parking. I hadn't parallel parked in years, maybe since flunking that part of the test both times as an adolescent. How in the hell was I going to do that now?

The emotional scars from my previous failures had run deep, I'd abandoned parallel parking as a 16-year-old and never embraced it again. Always opting to park further away, I was quick to point out to passengers that a little exercise never hurt anyone.

As someone who hadn't parallel parked in almost 40 years, I wasn't sure how the examiner would respond to the same "a little exercise never hurt anyone" mantra that my family and friends had tolerated. I'd have to go with the more conventional option. I'd have to try to parallel park.

I reconciled my concerns. Even if I flunked that part of the test, I could still do well enough to get my license.

Parking uphill. Parking downhill. It had been on the written exam. Wheels angled toward the curb. Wheels angled away from the curb.

And where was my parking brake?

Turn the radio off.

Lost in my thoughts, I hadn't seen the examiner approach my car. He entered the passenger door and introduced himself. "Hello. My name is Tru. I'll be administering your test today."

"Hi, Tru. It's good to meet you."

As Tru explained the forthcoming road test, I couldn't help but be distracted by the young driver beside me who had just departed for his road test and had turned into the wrong lane on his first left turn. That poor schmuck is toast, I thought. Sure enough, his test was aborted soon after it had started and he and his instructor drove into the parking lot across the street. OK, "dude", instead of flashing me the weird looks when I was testing my horn, maybe you should have noticed that the street directly in front of you was a two-way street.

At Tru's behest, I proudly displayed my vast knowledge of my equipment. Turn signals, windshield wipers, flashers, horn, lights. I was surprised that he didn't want to know how to work the radio or the CD player. Those were things I'd learned about the car immediately.

"Very good, Thomas. Any questions before we proceed?"

"No, I don't think so, Tru." Except if I flunk this test, will you explain to my family what a moron I am for driving around without a license for five years? Maybe you can think up some kind of excuse. Either way, it will be as good as anything I can come up with.

After a couple left turns, a couple right turns, some lane changes, and 90-degree backup parking, I felt like I was sailing through the test. OK, I'd almost obliterated a group of lollygagging pedestrians, but they scurried across the crosswalk when I honked my horn and flipped 'em the bird. Damn pedestrians. Didn't they know that I was in the middle of taking my driver's test?

Maybe three minutes into my road test, I spotted the orange cones that I'd been dreading.

"OK, Thomas. Now I'm going to ask you to parallel park between these cones."

"OK."

I pulled up adjacent to the front cones and backed in carefully, making sure not to hit any of the cones. Without any trouble, I maneuvered my Jeep into the pretend parking spot.

"Very good", said Tru.

Damn, if I'd have known that I could parallel park for the last 38 years, I wouldn't have had to walk so much.

Grinning like a Cheshire cat, I followed Tru's instructions and reluctantly vacated the territory I had just marked.

In the next two or three minutes, I made sure I didn't go through any stop signs, make any improper turns, exceed the speed limit, or lay any rubber. Now that I could parallel park, I was invincible.

When Tru finally told me to pull over to the curb, he wrote on the test form on his clipboard.

"OK, Thomas", he said when he finished writing. "You passed your test. The only thing you did wrong was that you didn't look both ways when we went through the green light. Even though the light was green, we caution you to look both ways before proceeding through the intersection. But other than that, everything was fine. You're good to go. If you'll take this exam sheet into the building, you'll be able to get your temporary license. Have a nice day."

"Thanks, Tru. Good to meet you." I didn't bother to tell him why I hadn't looked both ways at the intersection. I didn't bother to tell him that my neck was so stiff from old age that my head no longer turned. I couldn't be sure, but rigor mortis was probably beginning to set in.

Tru opened the door of my car and headed to the next driver.

Soon after he'd gone, it dawned on me that I didn't have anyone there to share in my triumph. It wasn't like I was 16 years old when I'd gone back to my dad with a shit-eating grin. I thought about asking Tru to come back to my car for a quick hug, but I wasn't sure how he felt about public displays of affection.

Either way, I was sure that I'd never again neglect to renew my driver's license. And when I got back to my office area, I'd head over to Grand Avenue for a late lunch and find a place where I could show off my newfound parallel parking skills.

Inchworm

I've read stories recently about the movement to ban dodge ball from schools in some states. I don't know how I feel about that. I got whacked in the head and other valuable areas a number of times during our 7th and 8th grade phy-ed classes. Supposedly, the dodgeballs that hit me in the head were errant, but then again most of those were thrown by Mr. Martin, the gym teacher.

Proponents of the dodgeball ban say the game promotes aggressiveness and bullying. They also say it causes humiliation and creates self-esteem issues. I don't think my experiences with dodgeball had any effect on my self-esteem, but it's hard to think about self-esteem when you're just happy to be alive after getting pasted by a big rubber ball.

But if you want to talk about humiliation in phy-ed class, at least for me, how about the rope climb? Freshman gym class. I remember the rope climb vividly. The emotional scars manifest themselves every time I start to feel good about myself.

Just a week after winning the contest for the most situps in Mr. Bjelland's phy-ed class, my classmates and I were introduced to the next part of our fitness challenge…the big thick rope with the bulbous knot on the end, hanging from the rafters of the high school gymnasium. Mr. Bjelland explained the techniques which would be needed for us to climb to the top of the rope as quickly as possible. Scurry up the rope, touch the metal rafter, scurry down the rope. Seemed easy enough.

Stopwatch in one hand, clipboard in the other, Mr. Bjelland called the names of the kids in the class and we took turns climbing the rope.

Some of the kids scampered up the rope in a manner that would have made Spiderman proud. Others reminded me of Rocky, Bullwinkle's flying squirrel friend. Some of the kids struggled, but eventually made it, egged on by the cheers of their classmates below. Marvin Eversman made it to the top, but then lost most of the skin from the palms of his hands as he slid down the rope, too exhausted to move his hands.

The gravity-challenged Chad Hessler made it halfway up the rope, before his progress was stymied. He hung there like a huge piece of tallow, as the rope swung back and forth like a pendulum. The miraculous burst of energy he'd hoped for never came, and when Mr. Bjelland told him to come down, he obliged.

Roger Meier made it, but in his haste to get back to the floor 25 feet below, he nearly lost his future ability to father little Meiers when he slid down the rope and his descent was bluntly interrupted by the knot on the bottom of the rope. Young Meier flopped to the padded mat below the rope and scrunched himself into the fetal position, his classmates and Mr. Bjelland entertained by his temporary misfortune.

When my turn came, near the end of the list, only Chad Hessler hadn't made it to the top. With biceps that could have starred in a spaghetti commercial, I huffed and I puffed and I made it only about a third of the way up the rope.

This exercise in futility continued every week before we played basketball. Eventually, only Chad Hessler and I were required to climb the rope, while all the other kids watched. In the fifth week, with all of his classmates exhorting him, Chad Hessler finally made it to the top, although with his size, some of the kids swore they saw the steel girders of the gymnasium bend. I should have been happy for him, but I wasn't. It was no longer me against Chad. It left me as the only person in gym class who hadn't made it to the top of the rope.

Two more weeks passed. I found myself dreading the thought of gym class, which had previously been my favorite class. Mr. Bjelland was now using a calendar instead of a stopwatch. The ceiling of the gymnasium was my Mount Everest. Mr. Bjelland, great motivator that he was, had even told the class that we wouldn't have to run laps after class "if Symalla ever makes it to the top".

Determined to finally make it, I moved slowly up the rope, ignoring my friend Mark Hedstrom, who sang his rendition of "Inchworm, inchworm. Measuring the marigolds. Seems to me you'd stop and see how beautiful they are."

After what seemed like hours, but was only minutes, I neared the top of the rope. Careful not to lose my grip, I reached for and touched the steel girder that held the rope. If I'd have had the stamina, I would have carved my initials in the damn thing, but, wearing a sheepish grin, I quickly scrambled down the rope . The other kids in the class were cheering for me, but mostly because they didn't have to run laps that day.

Emotional scars? I don't think so. Lessons learned? Sure. The rope climb reminded me that not everything comes easy. When I had won the situps contest, I hadn't shown a modicum of modesty. But that giant rope guided me back to reality. Secretly, I was proud of climbing that rope. Maybe I was embarrassed and humiliated, but sometimes life is like that. I was happy to know that I didn't quit. I eventually conquered, able to do something I wasn't sure I'd ever be able to do.

That being said, I don't think I'll ever get the role of Jack in "Jack and the Beanstalk". And given my current physique, I don't think I'll get the role of the beanstalk either.

Time In A Bottle

"Stick the dagger in and twist it", I encouraged V. "I'm friggin' thirsty."

Brimming with machismo, my compadre took a long drag on his Marlboro and then balanced it in a black plastic ash tray. "It's a done deal, T", he assured me as he summoned his weapon. Slowly, he chalked the tip of his cue, preparing the dagger, before voicing his intent. "Eight ball in the side, boys", he notified our opponents of their imminent demise.

Already conceding, one of our opponents was scouring his wallet for beer money; his partner was scraping the bottom of his jean pockets for the quarter they would need for an eventual rematch. From the juke box, Bob Seger's "Night Moves" framed the moment.

"Good job, partner", I nodded in satisfaction as V returned to the small round table which we'd designated as our perch for an impressive string of victories.

"We're en fuego tonight, T."

A couple of guys in our early twenties, Shane Venston and I had become fast friends at IDQ.

When we met, I was the only male among four women in the company's public relations department. The women I worked with were great. They were all older than me, but only by a couple of years. I was initially intimidated by the age, but not the gender. But eventually I realized that 24- and 25-year old women weren't much more worldly than a fresh-out-of-college 22-year-old guy. When new Dairy Queen franchisees toured our department, I'd introduce my associates as my secretaries. An entire stable of secretaries, I said, to transcribe all of the work I did and to fetch me coffee at my mere whim. That went over like a lead balloon with my female associates, but we all laughed about it nonetheless.

Despite my musings, I became good friends with my female PR associates. None of them took themselves too seriously, none of them took me seriously, and, as a result, we had lots of laughs. As the token male and the closest male at-hand, I was often asked to speak for the entire male gender, especially on matters of dating and social relationships. I always prefaced my opinions with, "Well, I'm certainly no expert, but…" and I then proceeded to speak at length for every man on the planet. I'll admit that I enjoyed the role and the attention, whether or not I knew what I was talking about.

In return, my female associates would sometimes indulge me by talking sports or feigning interest in my old college stories, which may have initially been amusing, but became a lot less interesting when I repeated them so frequently that my co-workers could eventually tell them better than I could.

On occasion, however, I needed a respite from the estrogen-enveloped environment of the IDQ PR department. The company's mail room and shipping room was only a short stroll down the hall and was a haven when I wanted to talk in-depth sports, women, and the same college stories of which my PR associates had grown weary.

Shane Ventson was a shipping clerk in the IDQ mail room. Almost immediately upon meeting, we found out that we shared a passion for baseball and it wasn't long before we became bleacher bums for many of the Twins games at nearby Met Stadium. The trunk of my baby blue Mercury, my dad's old company car, was soon christened as tailgate headquarters and became a permanent home to a small Char-Broil grill, a never-ending bag of Kingsford charcoal briquettes, dirty barbecue utensils, and a white styrofoam cooler.

Friends or co-workers who wanted to take in a ballgame with V and I were always welcome. The more, the merrier. "Just meet us under the Kansas City Athletics sign in the parking lot. That's the one with the picture of an elephant balancing himself on a big baseball. And BYOBBBBBB. Bring your own beer, brats, burgers, and broads. Or, if you're a broad, bring a boy, if you have one. If not, we can probably provide one, especially after the post-game refreshments."

Although V was married, he didn't have any kids and his wife Jill worked nights at her father's liquor store while she worked with no sense of urgency toward a yet to be determined degree at the U of M.

That left V with a lot of spare time and he and I became almost inseparable. Not only were we baseball buddies and pool partners, we were softball teammates and armchair philosophers.

V was one of the most personable people I had ever met, able to disarm just about any stranger within a matter of minutes without working at it. A golden personality. Bright, creative, sensitive, great sense of humor. Yet he worked as a shipping clerk and this bothered me much more than it did him.

"Why are you working in the mail room, V?", I asked him. "I realize it's none of my business. Nothing against the mail room or the guys who work there, but you have way too much talent to be sorting envelopes for the rest of your life."

"I don't know, T. You, Scottie, Digger, Bobby, Grant...you all went to college. If the Wizard of Oz hadn't been busted, maybe I could have asked him for one of those fancy college degrees that you guys used to get your jobs. While you guys were taking courses and cramming for tests, I was still trying to find myself. Unfortunately, I found myself at too many parties and without a college education."

"You've got to get over the college degree thing, V. You're hung up on it. It's just a slip of paper. It hangs over your head like a dark cloud and you're the only one who can see it. You're smarter than most of the people we work with. Oh, you're not as smart as me, but those were just the cards we were both dealt", I said with a wry smile as I swigged a bottle of Blatz. "There's a job opening in the marketing department. I think you should apply. I bet Gary would give you a shot at it. He knows how talented you are."

In late night alcohol-addled conversations, V and I often talked about the day we'd start our own business. We knew we weren't ready yet, but we both agreed that it would happen someday. We weren't sure what the business would be, but whatever it would be, we would work hard and have fun. We'd be next-door neighbors in a Bloomington cul-de-sac. Our wives would become best friends, our dogs would enjoy sniffing each other, and our kids would play sandlot baseball together. If they were boy and girl, they'd probably even go to the Jefferson prom together, and they'd have our permission to ignore the curfew that their moms had set.

It took me a while to warm up to V's wife Jill. It took her just as long to warm up to me. She was a serious save-the-world sort. I sometimes doubted that she wanted to be so serious, but that's just the way she was. Jill didn't like baseball, she was a klutz at pool, and she wasn't much for smalltalk or shoptalk. Jill and I faked friendliness whenever we were together, but when it came down to it, we had nothing in common except her husband and my best friend.

Our co-existence remained peaceful and passive until a summer night when I went to their apartment to help V move some furniture. He had been delayed, Jill informed me. He was at his parent's house helping his dad with something. Jill offered me a beer, and seemed surprised when I accepted. "It's a long walk back", I said, answering her look of surprise as to why I didn't retreat to my apartment in the adjacent apartment complex. She obviously hadn't expected me to stay. "I suppose I could take it to go", I tried to cover my tracks.

"No. No, please stay, Symalla."

In an awkward, but groundbreaking, conversation that night, Jill opened up. She revealed that she had often felt jealous of my friendship with her husband. She said she also felt jealous of some of V's other friends, but mostly with me. She acknowledged that I had more in common with her husband than she did and she was quick to admit her own shortcomings in this arena. Even when the three of us did something together, she always felt like the odd-person-out.

As Jill talked about V, I realized that she saw many of the same things in him that I did. She saw them as his wife and I saw them as his best friend, but we both saw his underlying talent and untapped potential.

From that night on, Jill and I became friends. We still didn't have much in common, but we had a newfound respect for each other. Conversations which had previously drip-dripped like a slow bottle of ketchup now flowed easily.

Jill became my biggest cheerleader and confidant in my new relationship with Cindy McGowan. Cindy was a summer intern who had been assigned to work in my department at IDQ. Bright and beautiful, funny and fetching, Cindy McGowan was way out of my league, if I even had a league. But for reasons unbeknownst to me, she liked me.

In awe of my own good fortune, I spent way too much time wondering why Cindy McGowan liked me.

In matters and discussions regarding Cindy McGowan, Jill was a good listener. I was well aware that Jill Ventson's serious nature wouldn't allow her to make fun of me. I also liked the fact that she didn't work at IDQ. In our conversations regarding Cindy, I had sworn Jill to secrecy, including with her husband. Even though Jill and I were new friends, I never doubted that she'd breach the trust I bestowed on her.

"I don't know, J. Sometimes I wonder if she's just selected me to break her summer boredom until she heads back to college in the fall." It was the same cynic in me that told me that Jill wanted my relationship with Cindy to work out, so she could finally spend more time with her husband. "But what if she is really interested, J? The signs are there. I think she really likes me. We've had a great time this summer, but she leaves for Gustavus in three weeks. What do I do then? I've never felt like this before."

Although Jill had never met Cindy, she was always quick to assure me that , from what I had told her and from what she knew about women, Cindy's interest was sincere.

When Jill and V and Cindy and I finally doubled, Jill got to meet the woman who had created so much of my consternation. When Cindy had excused herself to visit the ladies room at the Rusty Scupper, Jill was quick to relay her analysis. "Wow, T. You two have great chemistry. She's definitely a keeper, Symalla. There's no doubt, she really likes you." V, who was also enamored with Cindy McGowan, looked at Jill and I as if he was odd-person-out.

Months later, I felt like I'd been cold-cocked when V told me that he and Jill were getting a divorce. I experienced a gamut of emotions. Disbelief, anger, disappointment, sadness, hopelessness. I was speechless, sick to my stomach. I swore, then I pouted. When I got home, I turned on the television and stared at it without watching until the early hours of the morning. I was devastated. Maybe a better friend would have asked V for details on why he and Jill were calling it quits, but I didn't want to hear any of the reasons.

I'd always heard stories about how divorced couples would divide their mutual friends, who would feel compelled to make "Sophie's Choice" in selecting one of the two to continue their relationship with. Sadly, I knew that I'd end up being right about that. Jill and I exchanged Christmas cards the first year after the divorce. We said we would get together, but I knew we never would.

The last time I ever talked to Jill was before she had moved out of the house they had bought from V's grandmother. I had stopped by to see V, but he wasn't there that night. Jill and V had continued to live together while they made arrangements to go separate ways. This dissolution of their marriage was obviously civil.

"Take care of him, Symalla", she implored. "Just because he and I are getting a divorce doesn't mean I won't care about him any more. I'm sure he's told you why this is happening."

"No, J. Actually, he hasn't. And I'll be honest with you in telling you that I haven't asked. I keep thinking that maybe it's better if I don't know."

"You know he has a drinking problem, don't you?"

"Oh, I don't know about that. I'm out with him a bunch. He likes to have his beer, but I can't say that I've seen where he's ever had a problem. It's not like he's stumbling around or slurring his words. I don't think I've ever seen him where I've thought he's been too drunk to drive. He always seems to be under control. I wish I could say the same about myself."

"Well, maybe you don't know it, but his activities with you are usually just the start of his evening. You're his warm-up act. You don't see how much he drinks when he gets home."

"Oh, it can't be that much, can it? What, he has a beer or two when he gets home? Sometimes I like to have a nightcap when I get home. Are you talking about more than that, J?"

"A lot more than that, Symalla. Sometimes a 12-pack. Almost every night."

"Aw, come on, Jill. You must be padding that a bit. I see him at work in the morning and he never looks like he is hung over."

"Follow me", she said, leading me outside to their garage. Immediately, I saw the garbage cans full of empty beer cans and the stacked cases of beer bottles. The sheer quantity of the empty containers left me temporarily speechless. Jill was right. V drank too much.

"Jill, I never knew", I said in disbelief. "I honestly never knew."

"It's not your fault, Symalla. I just thought you ought to know."

" Wow. I never had any idea. Thanks for letting me know. How could I have missed this?"

At work, my prodding had paid off. V had cast aside his pretense about his lack of a college degree and had applied for the open position in the company's marketing department. After a brief interview process, he was awarded the job, which came with a nice salary increase and placed him on a career track where the absence of a college degree no longer mattered as much. He'd now be graded mostly on his performance and his ability.

V flourished in his new position. As I'd thought, he made a great field marketing rep. I was proud of him.

His concerns about not having a college degree still surfaced occasionally. One of the first times he traveled in his new marketing position, a 3M executive seated next to him on a flight almost destroyed his fragile psyche. The pretentious blowhard proceeded to tell V that even though he had secured a nice marketing job, he'd still have to get a college degree or he could never be successful. When V reluctantly told me this story, I could tell that he'd placed way more importance on this advice than it deserved.

"V, you already are successful", I reiterated, knowing full well that all the king's horses and all the king's men would have to work through the night to put Humpty Dumpty back together again.

I never got around to talking to V about the accumulation of empty Blatz containers in his garage. Soon after Jill had alerted me to the problem, I accepted a job with a restaurant chain in Dallas. I had not been looking to leave IDQ and I certainly hadn't been looking to leave Minnesota. IDQ was a good company, except for the skimpy paycheck, and Minnesota was home. But headhunters had beaten me down with offers of twice my salary or more, and, as a young guy driving a used car and barely making my rent, I finally succumbed to the continuous parade of offers.

No one, including V, had any idea that I was considering other employment. I didn't want the word getting around that I was looking at other opportunities, because I liked the job I had and because I wasn't sure if my desire to make more money would pass.

When I told V that I would be moving to Dallas at the end of the month, I had hoped he would be happy for me, but he didn't talk to me for two weeks.

Finally, a week before my move, I confronted him. "V, you don't understand. I'm going to make more than twice what I'm making now. How could I turn that down? It's a chance for me to finally get on my feet financially. I might want to have a family someday. I want to start my own business someday. I won't be able to do that on the money I'm making now."

"You're right, T. I just don't get it. You have everything going for you. A great job, tons of friends, a cool lady. How does it get any better than that?"

"V, I knew it was over last month when I had an interview with Burger King and Paul Enghauser offered me double the money for a job that basically consisted of arranging personal appearances for the Mystical Magical Burger King. Twice the money I'm making now to drive around a guy in a crown and a clown outfit. What does that say about the amount of money I'm making now?"

"Well, say what you want, Symalla. In my humble opinion, you're a money-grubbing pig. You're selling your soul. You know it and I know it. I want no part of it."

"It's only temporary, V. I've admitted I'm doing it for the money. But with all the extra money I'll be making, I'll be able to get the seed money for the business we've talked about starting. How else do you think we're going to be able to start our own business? Do you think the money is going to fall like manna from heaven? Or are you planning to hijack a Brinks truck? If we're going to have our own business, someone is going to have to step up. And I'm stepping up."

"What about the Twins?"

"I'll miss the Twins. I can't deny it. I'll miss the Twins."

"Who am I going to be able to call at 5:15 and get to go to a Twins game with me? Who's going to burn the taste out of the burgers on the grill and still think they're good? Who's going to be there with me when Mike Marshall pitches in his 100th game of the season?"

"Like I said, I'll miss the Twins."

"What about coaching little league?"

"Season's over. At least I'm not leaving in mid-season. Yes, I'll miss coaching the kids."

"And what about Cindy. How can you walk away from that? You're an idiot, Symalla. Seed money or no seed money, I'm pissed."

"Say what you want, Ventson. At least I have the balls to take the future into my own hands. You think it's easy for me to leave my friends? To leave you? To leave the Twins and the Vikes? To leave my little league kids? To leave Cindy? Well, it's not easy. Matter of fact, it's damn hard. But it's something I have to do."

The conversation carried on in a similar vein until it had played its course. It eventually softened, we agreed to disagree, and I shook hands with the best friend I'd ever had and headed home that August night.

When I returned to Minnesota from Dallas for the Thanksgiving holiday, I stayed at V's house before I headed home to Cold Spring to visit my parents and sisters. V introduced me to his new girlfriend, who was now living with him. Katrina was an old high school girlfriend who had moved to Aspen after graduation to be a ski instructor. Tired of the ski scene, she moved back to Minnesota after a couple of years. She and V reconnected after his divorce and fell in love.

Like a kid who had been a victim of the previous divorce, I tried not to like Kat, but she was imminently likeable. I was disappointed in how quickly I liked her, given my predisposition to V's first wife, Jill.

V and I talked into the wee hours of the morning during that visit. He seemed happy with his life and comfortable with the decision that we would remain good friends, even though we now lived over 1000 miles apart.

On frequent trips to Minnesota during my time in Dallas, I always got together with V. He and Kat married soon after they reunited , and Kat quickly became pregnant. V was excited at the prospect of being a father and we joked about how quickly his future son or daughter would be playing whiffle ball, running the bases, shagging fly balls.

When V and Kat had Jason, I was like a proud uncle.

Kat was always a welcoming and sincere host on my visits from Dallas. Although she wasn't at all like Jill, she quickly became someone I looked forward to seeing.

V's career was going well. Eventually, he too gave in to the barrage of calls from headhunters promising much more money for similar responsibilities. When he left IDQ to work for another Twin Cities-based restaurant chain, I informed him that he too was a money-grubbing pig.

"Yeah, yeah. Oink, oink. We're pen pals, I guess. I squeal every time I hoof it to the bank with my bigger paycheck", he responded with a smile. A rising star in his new company, he quickly climbed the corporate ladder to a director of advertising position.

"Not bad for a schmuck without a college degree", I joked with him when he told me of the promotion he'd earned.

That winter, on my way back to Dallas from a meeting in Grand Forks, bad weather in North Dakota had forced me to miss a connection in Minneapolis. I was stranded in the Cities for the evening and the airport was a zoo full of crabby travelers, so I called V to find out if he was doing anything. Kat answered the phone and informed me that V was in Wisconsin on business.

"But, you have to stop by, Symalla. I'm stranded here with Jason and I could use some company. Someone who doesn't talk babytalk, even though I realize that may be difficult for you. Have you eaten yet? I'm whipping up a batch of my world famous nachos."

"You're going to try to impress someone from Texas with your nachos? I'd say you have your work cut out for you, young lady. I'll be there in a couple of hours. I have to get a hotel room first and then I'll head over for some of your famous nachos."

"No. No time to get a hotel room. I'm absolutely famished. If you want some nachos, I suggest you get here soon. You can find a hotel room from here, or , if you want, you're welcome to the couch if you can get the cats off it."

Kat and I devoured the nachos and talked well into the night before I crashed on the couch. She was excited to be a mom; at the same time, she was enjoying her new career as an assistant manager at a local hotel. V was happy in his job as ad director, she said, but the travel was starting to get to him. More importantly, he was enjoying his role as a father. He couldn't wait until he could teach Jason to play baseball.

I had left my position as a promotions director for a restaurant chain and had gone to work for a Dallas ad specialty company. Ever since my days at IDQ, I'd been interested in imprinted promotion items. I was also enjoying my new career. V became one of my clients and we used our business relationship as an excuse to talk on a regular basis.

When V told me that he and Kat were getting a divorce, I was devastated again. Kat and Jason were moving to Washington, where Kat had a job managing a Ramada Hotel. "I really liked, Kat. You know you're a dope, don't you, V?"

Kat and I kept in touch for a brief period of time after she'd moved to the Northwest. She called a couple of times for gift items for her hotel staff. I was never quite sure if she really wanted the gift items or if she just wanted to talk. Either way, she bought some gift items and I told her multiple times that it was really good to hear from her again. V was doing OK, she said. He missed his son, but he hadn't contested their move to Washington.

It wasn't long before mutual friends informed me that V was struggling with his ad job. He was missing deadlines and he seemed overwhelmed and disinterested. I tried to broach the subject and find the root of the problem in some of our diminishing phone conversations, but he would never tell me what was going on, despite my poking and prodding. Miles away, with a friend who was reluctant to discuss his problems, I felt helpless.

After V was dismissed from his advertising position, we seldom talked. My calls were not returned. Eventually, his home phone was disconnected. Busy starting my own ad specialty company, I felt that I no longer had the time to chase an old friend who was slip-sliding out of my existence, and maybe his own existence.

In Dallas, I received occasional reports on my old friend. He worked for a furniture moving company, moving furniture. He was drinking heavily. He was in danger of losing his house. He'd flipped out, whatever that meant. He'd given up alcohol and found religion.

Mutual friends had tried to reach out to him, but had come away thinking that he was spiraling out of control. Mutual friends diagnosed that regardless of what was happening with V, he had become a shell of his former self. The bright, energetic, soulful, fun-loving friend we'd known had been gutted by his demons, whatever they were.

Although my sources were good, I decided not to pass judgment until I could see for myself. But, by the same token, I was in no hurry to see for myself. I was afraid of what I might see.

By the time I had moved back to Minnesota, I had heard that V was working for his brother-in-law's satellite toilet company.

His new profession offered lots of punch lines, but I found it hard to find humor in any of them.

For almost four months after my return to Minnesota, now running the company that V and I had dreamed of starting together, I thought often about calling him to let him know I was back in town. But I convinced myself that I was too busy establishing my business in Minnesota. When I finally surrendered to guilt and summoned the courage to call him, he appeared excited to hear from me and we agreed to get together for lunch the following week. He was anxious to show me the business where he was an operations manager, so I agreed to meet him at work, where he proudly gave me a tour before we headed to lunch.

We went to lunch at a nearby Perkins, where we both found it easier to chat with the middle-aged waitress than with each other. In our short reunion, we eventually updated each other on our lives. He was coordinating the portable satellites for Grand Old Days, the annual St. Paul street celebration. It was quite a task, he said, with over 200,000 people attending the one-day event and many of them having to use the facilities. He had been born-again, he said, but found it to be a bit extreme. He didn't drink anymore. I was glad and sad for that. Those days were now gone. Although our running-buddy activities had never revolved around alcohol, it had almost always been present. If abstinence from alcohol helped him piece his life back together, or maybe even save his life, I applauded his decision.

He was living with a lady named Becca and they had two kids together. They hadn't married, but they'd lived together for years now. He was a proud papa, eager to tell me about his kids. He hadn't been to a Twins game in years. The day they tore down Met Stadium was "the day the music died", he said, and he'd been to the Metrodome only once, for an '87 World Series game. We both now agreed with what our mothers had told us when we were growing up. Baseball was not meant to be played indoors.

Despite his aversion to the Metrodome, V still loved baseball. He managed and played for a 35-and-over baseball team and he coached his stepdaughter's softball team. She was a helluva player, he said.

He was anxious for me to meet Becca. They lived in the same house I had visited many times before when he had been married to Jill, then Kat. "We'll have you over for a barbecue", he planned.

I'm not sure, but maybe he could sense my lack of enthusiasm to meet Becca. The fact of the matter was that I'd grown close to both of his previous wives and I didn't want the emotional investment of losing a third friend to another divorce. The fact was that I'd grown weary.

V and I continued to talk and continued to do business, as I produced some embroidered caps and jackets for his satellite company. He had definitely changed, but I wasn't sure how much of that to attribute to time and how much to attribute to his previous struggles. I'd acknowledged that I'd changed also. In our conversations and occasional meetings, it became apparent that we would never have the friendship we once had. A number of times, he tried to get me to sub for his 35-and-over baseball team. But I was always busy. He tried a number of times to arrange that barbecue he'd talked about. But I was always busy.

When I called him one day at the satellite company, they informed me that they were sorry, "Mr. Ventson is no longer with the company."

I tried to call him at home, but his phone was again disconnected. Over the course of the next few weeks, mutual friends told me that V had fallen off the wagon again. Concerned friend that I was, I never bothered to track him down to make sure he was OK. His phone number had been disconnected, but I still had his parents' phone number and his brother's phone number in my Rolodex.

Months later, he called me.

"You OK?", I asked. "I called you at work and they said you were no longer with the company. I called you at home and your phone was disconnected."

"Yeah, it's a long story. I won't bother you with the details. I'm working at Bruegger's Bagels in downtown Minneapolis now."

"You're managing a Bruegger's? One of my customers at The Barbers just left her job to join the Bruegger's management program. I hear they're a good company to work for."

"Well, they are a good company to work for, but I'm not managing the place. I'm an hourly employee. Serving bagels to the glitz and glamour crowd of downtown Minneapolis. After all the previous jobs I had, T, I realized that I wanted the least possible amount of responsibility. I got tired of all the stress. I know you won't understand, but that's just the way it is."

When I had worked at a Dallas restaurant chain, my friend John Kissane and I often joked that there were days when the job working the Jack-in-the-Box drive-thru looked very attractive. But we never acknowledged that the Jack-in-the-Box drive-thru probably wasn't any less stressful than the coat-and-tie ad gigs we had. And the drive-thru job at a fast food joint definitely didn't produce the paycheck to which we'd grown accustomed.

Now, my friend V was living the life we'd joked about. I was running the company we had hoped to start someday. He was slinging bagels. It's strange how things turn out sometimes.

At the end of the conversation from Bruegger's that day, V and I agreed to get together soon. But I knew we never would. That was my decision, not his. After all, he had reached out and I had backed away.

As I hung up the phone that day, I thought about friends, relatives, and acquaintances who had suffered tragic deaths when they were much too young. A boyhood friend was hit and killed by a car when riding a bicycle back from a party when we were in high school. A high school friend lost her parents and two siblings to a car accident and became an instant "mom" to her remaining siblings. My aunt Mary had died of breast cancer, leaving four young children behind. A fellow boxing aficionado died in a freak motorcycle accident. A 28-year-old client drove drunk into a bridge abutment on her way home from a party. A tennis partner died of a heart attack in the middle of a tennis match. A close friend was stabbed to death as he worked after-hours to print an order of t-shirts.

All of these people died much too young. I shed tears and shared heartfelt moments for all of them.

That being said, it's disappointing to note that I've yet to shed a tear for the best friend I've ever had. I'm not sure why this is. As I write this story, I'm not sure if Shane Ventson is dead or alive. Mutual friends have all lost touch. I'm embarrassed to admit that I haven't reached out to locate my best friend ever in a time and age when the internet makes it easy to do so. I'll admit that these failings might say more about me than it says about him. But, I'll also admit that I'm afraid of what I'll find.

As I've grown older, I've learned that if often hurts more to lose a friend who is still alive than it is to lose a friend who dies. There is finality in death. There is closure in death. With friends who die, you can remember them for all the good things they did in life. You can forget many of their shortcomings.

But for a lost friend who may be dead, who may be alive, I have a sense of guilt, a sense of conscience, a sense of responsibility. Maybe I should have helped, but didn't. Maybe I should have called, but didn't. Maybe I should have cared, but didn't. Maybe. Maybe. Maybe.

Demon of the Deep

I have friends in the South who marvel at the concept of ice fishing. They're baffled and befuddled by the idea of up to 10,000 people standing on the same sheet of ice to participate in an ice fishing contest…the thought of people driving their cars or trucks on lakes with plowed roads, street signs, and miniature neighborhoods…the thought of ice fishing houses outfitted with couches, bunk beds, microwave ovens, and satellite television service.

Anyone who has seen the movie "Grumpy Old Men" should have a much better grasp of the concept of ice fishing.

Countless Minnesotans wile away their winters on one of the state's 10,000 lakes, fishing in the varying comforts of ice houses …or on the open ice, if the weather is warm enough or if they've had enough peppermint schnapps.

Me? I've never been much of an ice fisherman. I'm not really sure how much this has to do with an experience I had as a 13-year-old kid.

As a kid, my dad would sometimes take me ice fishing. We never discussed why he took me fishing, but I suspect he did it because it allowed him to avoid some of the weekend chores my mom had designated for him. I would guess that I was probably part of the negotiations. When my dad agreed to take me with, my mom was always quick to agree that fishing would be OK.

With me out of the house, my mom wouldn't have to spend her time refereeing the tag team wrestling bouts between my younger sisters and I.

Even before the incident, I never relished the thought of ice fishing much. I was a wiener when it came to cold weather. And ice fishing and cold weather go hand-in-hand. Just the year before, I had frozen my ear, the same one Sister Arlene had taken a liking to in second grade. On my walk home from school, I had decided that I was too cool to wear a stocking cap. When my ear turned assorted shades of purple and black in the following weeks, I definitely wasn't too cool as I wore my stocking cap in class to hide the hideous-looking appendage on the side of my apparently empty noggin.

When I had first tried to wear the stocking cap in class, Sister Elise had reminded me that we weren't allowed to wear caps in school. But she eventually made an exception when she realized that my damaged ear was a distraction for the rest of the students. Also, she acknowledged that she didn't like looking at my ear either.

I was scared to death that my ear was going to fall off. At school, I'd be known as a young Vincent Van Gogh. At home, I'd be forced to view my lost ear in a pickle jar resting on the family fireplace mantel. It would be a daily reminder that I should have worn my stocking cap.

But my ear never fell off and it eventually returned to regular color.

From the time it froze, I was always aware that it was apt to freeze again, more quickly than it had before. Despite these concerns, I would always go ice fishing with my dad and I was always anxious to brag to my sisters that Dad had taken me fishing and not them.

The setting on the day it happened was Schneider Lake, a small link on the Chain of Lakes between Cold Spring and Richmond. We didn't have a fish house, but my Uncle Al had one that was set up on Schneider Lake. He had to cut hair that day and he had told my dad and I that we were welcome to use his fish house.

Uncle Al's fish house was a dark house, a small shanty with a big hole, used mostly for spearing northern pike.

It was a mild day. My dad had been reluctant to drive his car out on the ice ever since one of the men in town had lost his car to ice that wouldn't hold it. So we loaded our fishing gear on a toboggan and trudged through the snow to get to the fish house. I was always surprised to see that I could sweat in such cold temperatures.

After Dad had used the auger and the chisel to cut through the more than two feet of ice to create a rectangular hole in the fish house, and after he got the kerosene stove going, he announced that he would leave the fish house to me while he fished outside on the open ice.

I agreed with the plan. The fish house was the size of an outhouse and it would be crowded with the both of us.

I pulled out the spear that my grandpa had made for me. I made sure I tied the spear's rope to the leg of my chair. If I threw my spear at a fish, I didn't want to worry about losing it to the bottom of the lake. Dad had told me about one of the men in town who had forgot to tie his spear to his leg or his chair. When he was unable to retrieve the spear on the bottom of the lake, he had to borrow a large magnet from Wenner's Hardware. Grandpa would really be disappointed if I lost the spear he made for me. I didn't want to pull a stunt like that.

Preparing for an afternoon of fishing, I lowered the new decoy my dad and I had made into the water. Dad had carved the decoy from a piece of pine, adding tin fins that would allow the decoy to navigate the water like it was swimming. He had allowed me to paint it. I had used the brightest colors available to create one of the most psychedelic decoys ever. Inspired by an Iron Butterfly album cover and playing "In-A-Gadda-Da-Vida" over and over again on the phonograph, I had created a decoy that fish were sure to notice. They'd probably need to wear sunglasses if they were going to visit this decoy, I had mused.

When Dad told me that he thought my decoy was too bright, I was quick to point out that Wally Westrum's dad had told him he was crazy when he baited his fishing hook with Cheetos.

"Fish won't bite on Cheetos", Wally's dad had told Wally.

"Well, they're not biting on anything else we've been using", Wally had responded.

When Wally quickly pulled in a fish with his cheese curl, Mr. Westrum hadn't said much other than "I'll be damned". When Wally got a second fish with a cheese curl, a smiling Mr. Westrum asked Wally to "Pass the Cheetos, please."

Thinking about my neon colored decoy, I was quick to tell my dad, "You just wait and see. I expect it won't be long before some of the guys in town start asking us where they can buy these psychedelic decoys." My dad didn't know what psychedelic meant.

After I had hung the decoy into the water, and after I admitted that I was surprised that the fish hadn't already started to shag it, I located the plastic bag of eggshells in my parka pocket. Grabbing a handful of crushed shells in one hand and my spear in the other hand, I dumped the eggshells into the water, hoping that the flash of the falling white flakes would look like a school of minnows to hungry fish. When the floating eggshells didn't produce the activity I had hoped, I resolved myself to the thought that once they rested on the bottom of the lake, the eggshells would at least make it easier for me to see the dark-bodied fish that would be coming to visit my psychedelic decoy.

After what may have been half an hour, it became obvious to me that my new neon decoy wasn't going to be the aquatic landmark I had hoped it would be. I shifted my thoughts to eighth grade basketball.

Despite countless hours of shooting baskets in the driveway that past summer, I hadn't been able to secure a starting spot on the basketball team. Mark Steil and John Dorgan had beat me out for the starting guard spots. Even though I may have been a better shot than my two counterparts, Mr. Seguin had pointed out that they were better all-around players. They were better at defense, they were better passers, and they were better at driving to the basket. Unfortunately for me, Mr. Seguin was right.

Next year, with the influx of players from Richmond, Rockville, and Watkins, I might not even make the team. Dickie

Rausch from Richmond was really good and he would be sure to get one of the starting guard spots. And with all the other forwards and centers coming in from the other towns...Jon Mueller, Greg Dols, Pat Benoit, Mike Loesch, I'd be lucky to be team water boy.

If only I had started playing basketball when all the other kids started playing. If only I was taller. If only I was quicker. If only I could jump. If only, if only, if only. My days of playing organized basketball were probably almost over.

Slowly, but surely, the smell of the kerosene stove began to induce a mid-afternoon nap. If I couldn't make the basketball team in real life, maybe I could make it in my dreams.

My head bobbed up and down as I half-heartedly resisted the inevitable. Floating in and out of consciousness, my mind drifted into one of those areas where it's difficult to tell real from surreal. I was content and comfortable, almost as if I'd just finished stuffing myself with Thanksgiving dinner. The clear water in the fishing hole was hypnotic.

Just as I had finally drifted into oblivion, the big black furry creature blasted through the fishing hole. Jarred back to reality, my heart stopped beating as I jumped to my feet.

"Holy shit", I screamed. "Holy shit."

In the dark of the fish house, I couldn't tell what the big black furry creature was, but its bright yellow eyes let me know that the Demon of the Deep had come to visit.

Grabbing for my spear, trying to focus on the creature who had erupted through the fishing hole, I slipped and fell to the floor, dropping my spear. Immediately the big black creature was hovering over me, panting furiously. Curled up in the fetal position, I told myself that this was it. This is it, I said. I'm going to die. I'm going to die.

My dad opened the door of the fish house. "What's going on in here?"

When I finally removed my arms from covering my head, the big black dog on top of me was trying to lick my face. After he had shook off the cold water from which he had just emerged, he answered my dad's query by wagging his tail and letting out a friendly yelp. I, on the other hand, checked my underwear. Thankfully, no deposits.

Before I got a chance to tell my dad what happened, another fisherman made his way over to our fish house. He formally introduced us to his black lab, Big Ben, named after the TV show with the big black bear.

Apparently, Big Ben had been fishing with his owner when he decided to go after a fish the man had hooked. All hell broke loose and Big Ben got under the ice and couldn't find his way back to the fishing hole he'd jumped into. In danger of drowning, he'd been fortunate enough to spot my fishing hole, from where he emerged unannounced.

We had a black lab at home and I loved labs. Blackie and Big Ben were kindred spirits, I thought. This was something that Blackie would have done.

But I doubt that Big Ben or his owner understood the aftereffects of that Saturday afternoon. From that day on, a fish house was never a good place to take a nap.

About the Author

As a colicky baby, the author was wrapped in swaddling clothes and abandoned in a wicker basket along the banks of the Sauk River in Cold Spring, Minnesota. He was soon discovered by a curious pack of brush wolves, who raised him as one of their own for three years before realizing that he ate too much. The wolves eventually returned Symalla to his birth parents, who took him back only because they had no other options.

Symalla traded household chores for food and shelter throughout his childhood. As an adult, Symalla remembers his time as a wolf with fondness. On occasion, he is still known to bay at the moon, a notion which is usually preceded and enhanced by a couple of Budweisers.

Symalla's real family first discovered his interest in writing one Sunday afternoon when they were entertaining relatives. On that day, the eight-year-old future author sent out an S.O.S. to his relatives, using mixed vegetables on his dinner plate to write, "Help! I'm being held captive!" Wisely, the young man's relatives ignored his plea for help. They didn't want him either. Aggravated by their young son's feeble escape attempt, Symalla's parents immediately banned rescue-me-please pleas when the family had company.

Symalla attended St. Boniface Grade School in Cold Spring, where the Sisters of St. Benedict passed him from grade to grade like a hot potato. One of the nuns was heard to sing, "I don't want him. You can have him. He's too much for me."

The author graduated from Rocori High School in Cold Spring before enrolling at the College of St. Thomas in St. Paul, where he thinks he might have spent the best years of his life as a freshman, although he admits that it was a bit of a blur. He eventually graduated with a degree in journalism, a degree the College is still reluctant to recognize except when it's asking for money.

Symalla currently resides in St. Paul, where he owns a promotional products company.

7702462R0

Made in the USA
Charleston, SC
01 April 2011